The Hamas Massacre and the Transmutation of Antisemitism

The massacre of Israelis by Hamas terrorists on October 7, 2023, was the most dreadful slaughter inflicted upon the Jews since the Nazi Holocaust. In the immediate aftermath, Israel found itself fighting an existential war on seven fronts. The Western world might have been expected to rally behind Israel – the only liberal representative democracy in the Middle East. However, progressive public opinion in the West, in academia and among student bodies, the left of centre press, radio, and TV, all turned upon Israel in a tidal wave of anti-Zionism. Israel was itself accused of genocide and crimes against humanity. This was a modern form of medieval antisemitic blood libels. What was distinctive about this novel transmutation of antisemitism was that it was left-wing, post-modernist, neo-Marxist. It was the denial of the very legitimacy of the State of Israel. Hacker offers illuminating explanations of this puzzling phenomenon. The International Court of Justice and the International Criminal Court both condemned Israel for violations of international law – decisions that were demonstrably biassed and illicit. Hacker's meticulously researched discussion unravels the history of the Israel/Palestinian conflict, describes the successive Israeli offers of a Palestinian state on the West Bank that were rejected by corrupt Palestinian leaders who betrayed their own people, tells the sorry history of the Gaza Strip and the death-cult ideology of its elected Hamas rulers, analyses the commonly misunderstood requirements of international law, scrutinizes the pivotal role of the Iranian theocratic state in the war, and probes beneath the glib demand for recognition of a Palestinian state. This book will appeal to those interested in the Hamas massacre, the Gaza war, the Israel/Hezbollah war, and Iran/Israel war, antisemitism and its history, anti-Zionism and left-wing intellectuals in the West.

P. M. S. Hacker is Emeritus Fellow in Philosophy, St. John's College, Oxford, UK.

Studies in Contemporary Antisemitism

Series editors

David Hirsh, *Senior Lecturer in Sociology, Goldsmiths, University of London, and Academic Director of the London Centre for the Study of Contemporary Antisemitism*

Philip Spencer, *Emeritus Professor in Holocaust and Genocide Studies at Kingston University, and Visiting Professor in Politics at Birkbeck, University of London*

John Strawson, *Professor Emeritus of Law at the University of East London*

Beverley Brown, *Editor*

Published in conjunction with the London Centre for the Study of Contemporary Antisemitism, *Studies in Contemporary Antisemitism* is a timely, multidisciplinary book series, drawing primarily, but not exclusively, on the social sciences and the humanities. The series encourages academically rigorous and critical publications across several disciplines and that are explicit in understanding and opposing the presence and ascendancy of contemporary antisemitism in both its theoretical and empirical manifestations. The series provides a unique opportunity to offer an intellectual home for a diversity of works that, taken together, crystallize around the study of contemporary antisemitism. The series consists of research monographs, edited collections and short form titles.

Responses to 7 October
Law and Society
Edited by Rosa Freedman and David Hirsh, with Odeliya Lanir Zafir

Responses to 7 October
Universities
Edited by Rosa Freedman and David Hirsh, with Odeliya Lanir Zafir

The Hamas Massacre and the Transmutation of Antisemitism
P. M. S. Hacker

For more information about this series, please visit: www.routledge.com/studies-in-contemporary-antisemitism/ book-series/SICA

The Hamas Massacre and the Transmutation of Antisemitism

P. M. S. Hacker

Routledge
Taylor & Francis Group

LONDON AND NEW YORK

Designed cover image: 'Inferno' by P.M.S. Hacker

First published 2026
by Routledge
4 Park Square, Milton Park, Abingdon, Oxon OX14 4RN

and by Routledge
605 Third Avenue, New York, NY 10158

Routledge is an imprint of the Taylor & Francis Group, an informa business

© 2026 P. M. S. Hacker

For Product Safety Concerns and Information please contact our EU representative GPSR@taylorandfrancis.com. Taylor & Francis Verlag GmbH, Kaufingerstraße 24, 80331 München, Germany.

British Library Cataloguing-in-Publication Data
A catalogue record for this book is available from the British Library

ISBN: 978-1-041-19477-4 (hbk)
ISBN: 978-1-041-19473-6 (pbk)
ISBN: 978-1-003-71195-7 (ebk)

DOI: 10.4324/9781003711957

Typeset in Times New Roman
by Newgen Publishing UK

Contents

Preface

I am not a political scientist or a Middle East historian. I am an academic philosopher, a specialist in the philosophy of Wittgenstein on whom I have written a dozen books, and on philosophy and neuroscience on which subject I have, together with a great Australian neuroscientist Max Bennett, written four books. In recent years I have dedicated my energies to writing a tetralogy on human nature. What then has brought me to the point of writing a monograph on the 2023 Hamas massacre in Israel, on anti-Zionism and antisemitism? Largely indignation and revulsion at the falsehoods, lies, and hysterical demonstrations against Israel in its war with Hamas in Gaza, especially among the educated youth at universities and intellectuals across Europe, the USA and the antipodes. Anti-Zionism, as exhibited in recent years, readily morphs into antisemitism – an ancient moral and intellectual disease in Western culture. It is advanced by people who like to think of themselves as 'progressive' and 'liberal', many of whom enjoy the self-righteousness typical of antisemitism throughout the ages. Criticism of the policies of the State of Israel is perfectly legitimate. So is criticism of its government and Prime Minister Benyamin Netanyahu – at which Israelis excel. But criticism is quite distinct from delegitimization of the State of Israel – denying the right of the State of Israel to exist. That is anti-Zionism, and that, as I shall argue, is a form of antisemitism. Anti-Zionism was, to be sure, coordinated with Muslim antisemitism on the streets of Europe, the USA and Canada, as well as Australia. These huge weekly demonstrations were anything but spontaneous. They were coordinated, planned, and paid for primarily by extraneous organizations. Evidence will be adduced to confirm this.

I am a Jew, an atheist Jew. My parents came to Britain in 1928. My father, Emerich Hacker, was Hungarian – a doctor, who had studied medicine in Leipzig, where he met my mother, and had done his internship in Magdeburg. Fortunately for me and my older sister, he disliked Germany and was an Anglophile. I was born in London in 1939. When I was 11-years old, my parents were divorced and I went, with my mother and sister, to the recently created State of Israel, to join her aged father and two younger sisters who had emigrated from Germany to the British Mandate of Palestine in the 1930s. I spent ten years in Israel (1950–60). Almost by accident, I came back to England to study philosophy at Oxford. I fell in love with philosophy. I was fortunate to be taught for my doctoral degree by a truly great legal philosopher, H. L. A. Hart. Altogether by accident, I met my future wife, Sylvia, during my undergraduate years, and fell in love with her. We married and lived together for 59 years. A career in Oxford, at a time when Oxford was the greatest philosophical centre in the Western world, seemed bliss indeed, and when the opportunity came, I seized it and became a tutorial fellow in philosophy at St John's College. I did not lose contact with Israel. Indeed, in the early 1990s, Isaiah Berlin asked me to serve on the Rothschild Fellowship Committee for post-doctoral overseas fellowships at Yad Hanadiv in Jerusalem. For the next 19 years, I visited Israel every spring to participate in interviews and usually spent ten days to a fortnight there. I am now too aged to travel that far.

The Hamas massacre on October 7, 2023, should have shocked everyone. The response of the Israeli armed forces should have received the warmest support from the governments of the Western world and from the public. After all, the massacre was horrific – the most horrific slaughter of Jews since the Nazi Holocaust. Furthermore, Israel was and is the sole liberal representative democracy in the whole of the Middle East and North Africa. The Hamas slaughterers had violated and continued to violate every principle of international law, were guilty of genocide, and of crimes against humanity. Israel found itself fighting an existential war on seven fronts: Hamas in the Gaza Strip, Hezbollah (an Iranian proxy) in south Lebanon; Syria (ruled by the mass murderer Assad); terrorist groups embedded in the West Bank (Judaea and Samaria) under the aegis of Mahmoud Abbas; the Houthis in Yemen; Iraqi terrorist groups that fired whatever long-range rockets they could at Israel; and behind all these, the theocratic Islamic Republic of Iran – sworn to the destruction of the State of

Israel and intent on achieving regional super-power status. Surely western governments would rally behind Israel?! Surely the public would demonstrate in support of this tiny, embattled state, no larger than Wales?! But exactly the opposite happened.

In my own university, Oxford, on October 20, 2023, within days of the October massacre of October 7, when the Israeli armed forces had begun to attack Hamas, 42 Oxford academics, including philosophers, lawyers and political scientists, signed an Open Letter addressed to the Prime Minister Rishi Sunak and leader of the opposition Keir Starmer. In it they claimed that Israel was embarked on a 'morally disastrous exercise' (fulfilling the first obligation of any govern-ment – to defend the lives of their citizens?), accusing Israel of 'an unprecedented human catastrophe' (worse that the Holocaust? than Hiroshima? than the Holodomor?), of 'an affront to human dignity' (is defending one's citizens from deadly attack an affront to dignity?), and the adoption of typical terrorist policy of collective punishment (as if fighting against Hamas, who were continuing to fire rockets into Israel, were itself a form of terrorism). This shocked me, and I replied to this Open Letter, which had not even mentioned Hamas and its mur-derous attack on Israel. The correspondence, on the web, extended to a number of exchanges.

Oxford academia continued to distinguish itself in a like manner in 2024 in the person of Jeff MacMahon, an American professor of moral philosophy at Oxford, who fancies himself as a philosophical theorist of just wars even though he appears to be ignorant of the concept of proportionality in international law concerning collateral civilian deaths and injuries in fighting a war to defeat an invader. We shall examine this concept of proportionality below. McMahon argues that whereas Ukraine's war against Russia is a paradigm of a just war, Israel's war against Hamas's genocidal onslaught is not a just war at all[1] (*Analyse & Kritik* 2024). A spirited reply was published by Daniel Statman in *Analyse & Kritik* 2025 (47(1)), pp. 179–207. McMahon excels in the application of double standards and distortion of the facts.

This monograph is a continuation of my altercation with Oxford academics. Antisemitism has been said to be a canary in the coalmine of society – a measure of the corruption and degeneration of the social order and of social and political morality. The late Lord Jonathan Sacks, the Chief Rabbi of the Commonwealth, sapiently remarked, 'The hate that begins with the Jews never ends with the Jews. ... Antisemitism is the world's most reliable warning sign of the danger of a major threat to freedom, humanity, and the dignity of difference.' Antisemitism commonly presages the rise of totalitarian and authoritarian regimes of left- or right-wing persuasion. Fighting antisemitism is therefore a matter of great moment. To be sure, the hated are unlikely to be able to influence the haters. But bystanders, who are not well-equipped to follow the murky and convoluted events of the Middle East, who have no knowledge of international law, who glean most of their information from the left of centre British press and the BBC or from the leading US newspapers and journals, may find this book informative and perhaps even illuminating, even though what is illuminated is often terrible. What I have to offer is carefully collected information from sources as reliable as I could find, and reasoned argument. The arguments I advance are complex. It may be helpful to draw attention in advance to some of the salient points.

First, the antisemitism that has been unleashed by the Gaza War and the Israeli existential seven-front struggle for survival is a transmutation of an ancient hatred. It is left-wing antisemitism or neo-Marxist antisemitism, dressed up in the guise of anti-Zionism. This is a leitmotif of my investigations. To explain how this has come about is one of my purposes. My explanations are advanced in the penultimate chapter of the book.

Second, this left-wing antisemitism has been coordinated with traditional Muslim antisemitism. The massive anti-Israel, pro-Palestinian and pro-Hamas demonstrations have been funded by Qatar and Iran, and supported by Russia. To be sure, innumerable Muslims living in Britain and Europe may be more or less indifferent to events in the Middle East. But many, especially among the younger generation, are not. Antisemitism in Muslim societies has a long history and is embedded in foundational Islamic doctrine. It is important to be aware of this and not to be deluded by tales of happy coexistence and tolerance throughout the ages. It is a myth that before the British Mandate in Palestine was set up by the League of Nations, Jews lived happily side by side with Muslims in the Middle East and North Africa. Islam commenced with a massacre of Jews (in Medina). It incorporated anti-Jewish sentiments into its sacred writings. According to Islamic law, Jews were given *dhimmi* status as second-class people, were required to pay special taxes, and wear distinctive, identifying clothing. They were banned from government service and forbidden to build new houses of worship. They were periodically subjected to public humiliation. At certain periods, in Muslim lands, the Jews prospered and flourished, most famously, under the Umayyad Caliphate in Andalusia. But that flourishing was destroyed by the invasions of the Almoravids and subsequently the even more intolerant Almohads. Similarly, under Ottoman rule, there were periods of relative tolerance and periods of terrible persecution. Just how appalling Jewish life could be under Islamic rule is vividly depicted in George Orwell's essay 'Marrakesh':

> When you go through the Jewish quarters you gather some idea of what medieval Jewish ghettoes were probably like. Under their Moorish rulers the Jews were only allowed to own land in certain restricted areas, and after centuries of this kind of treatment they have ceased to bother about overcrowding. Many of the streets are less than six feet wide, the houses are completely windowless, and sore-eyed children cluster everywhere in unbelievable numbers, like clouds of flies. Down the centre of the street there is generally running a little stream of urine.
>
> In the bazar huge families of Jews, all dressed in long black robe and little black skull-cap, are working in dark fly-infested booths that look like caves. A carpenter sits cross-legged at a prehistoric lathe, turning chair-legs at lightning speed. He works the lathe with a bow in his right hand and guides the chisel with his left foot, and thanks to a lifetime of sitting in this position, his left leg is warped out of shape. ... .
>
> You hear the usual dark rumours about Jews, not only from the Arabs, but from poorer Europeans. "Yes, *mon vieux*, they took my job away and gave it to a Jew. The Jews! They're the real rulers of this country, you know. They've got all the money. They control the banks, finance, everything."
>
> (*Collected Essays,* vol. 1, pp.389–90)

The terrible persecution of Jews in Ottoman Palestine in the eighteenth and nineteenth centuries is described in detail in Avraham Yaari's *The Goodly Heritage* (Israel, 1958).

> On encountering a Jew in the street, an Arab would order him to pass on his left (since Satan stands on the Believer's left side). Woe betide the Jew if he so much as touched the Arab in passing. The latter would set upon him and proclaim that he had cursed Islam, whereupon a mob would gather and belabour the Jew who would end up with imprisonment and torture. In the market-place a Jew

was liable to be beaten, have stones thrown at him, have his beard pulled or be spat upon. ... Jews were stoned and mocked when they went to visit their sacred tombs or pray at the Wailing Wall. No Jewish woman dared venture abroad.

(p.46)

Modern Muslim antisemitism in the Middle East is not rooted merely in Islamic texts and in the customs of centuries, but has been fostered and cultivated by Nazi propaganda, on the one hand, and by Russian antisemitic propaganda, on the other. *Mein Kampf* and *The Protocols of the Elders of Zion* are best sellers in most Islamic states.

Third, it is a mistake to suppose that Zionism originated with the Balfour Declaration. It did not even originate with Theodore Herzl, although he made it into a vibrant practical movement. In one sense, it was embedded in the hearts and minds of diaspora Jewry ever since they had been exiled from their homeland in Judaea by Vespasian and subsequently by Hadrian. For every Passover celebration is accompanied by the prayer of longing: 'Next year in Jerusalem'. In another sense, Herzl was anticipated by Moses Hess in 1862, who advocated secular Zionism in his book *Rome and Jerusalem*. Zionism is patent in George Eliot's philosemitic novel *Daniel Deronda* (1876). Leon Pinsker was a founder of the early Zionist movements *Hibbat Zion* (*Love of Zion*) in 1881 and of *Hovevei Zion* (*Lovers of Zion*) in 1884, members of which were among the *First Aliyah* (immigrants to Zion) from the 1880s to the 1910s to the Ottoman Sanjaks of Jerusalem, Balqa, Acre and Beirut. Zionism was not the product of the Balfour Declaration but of the longing of a people for their ancient homeland.

Fourth, Hamas is a fanatical terrorist organization. Its aim is the annihilation of the State of Israel and the slaughter of its citizens. Its antisemitism was written into its original 1988 Charter. Article 22 runs:

With their money [the Jews] took control of the world media, news agencies, the press, publishing houses, broadcasting stations and others. ... They were behind the French Revolution, the Communist Revolution, and most of the revolutions we hear about. With their money they form secret societies, such as Free Masons, Rotary Clubs, the Lions and others. ... They were behind World War I, when they were able to destroy the Islamic Caliphate, making financial gains ... they were behind World War II through which they made huge financial gains by trading armaments.

It is, as will be shown, a *jihadist* death-cult. It is funded by Qatar and Iran. Its words are no more trustworthy than the words of the Kremlin. The value of truth, for Hamas, is not as a precondition of a human community. It is purely pragmatic – what one says is not presumed to be true unless proved otherwise, it is what is most useful to one's goals.

Fifth, it was Hamas that assaulted Israel on October 7, 2023. It aimed at the annihilation of as many Israeli citizens as possible and coordinated with Hezbollah in southern Lebanon. Israel did not begin this war. Israel was fighting a war of self-defence on multiple fronts.

Sixth, the mastermind of the war against Israel that aimed at its annihilation was the theocratic Islamic Republic of Iran. Iran, whenever it could, fought a proxy war, making good use of Hamas, Hezbollah, Houthis in Yemen, Syria under Assad, as well as terrorist groups on the West Bank. It also fired large salvos of long-range rockets and drones at Israel.

Seventh, in the 75 years of its troubled history, Israel has had to fight numerous wars. Its enemies aimed not to create an Arab Palestinian state, but to destroy Israel and to annihilate Jews. This was patent in the Israeli War of Independence. It was equally clear in the 1956 Sinai campaign, which Israel fought in order to put a halt to the fedayeen murderers sent by Nasser from Egypt to massacre Jews. It was obvious in the Six-Day War in June 1967, when Nasser on May 26 declared that 'our basic objective will be to destroy Israel' and made no mention of establishing a Palestinian state. In the 1973 Yom Kippur War, Sadat was not concerned with establishing a Palestinian state, but with ending the war of attrition across the Suez Canal that had been simmering over the previous three or four years to the great disadvantage of Egypt, its citizens, and its military. His aim was to defeat Israel, not to establish a Palestinian state. The Palestinian issue was *primarily* a rallying cry for Arab leaders, and a means of distracting their own populations from their dire socio-economic circumstances. There is nothing like hatred to inspire the enthusiasm of dictators, autocrats, and religious fanatics.

Eighth, the Palestinian Arabs (unlike the Palestinian Jews) have been singularly unfortunate in their leaders. There is an unbroken line from Amin Husseini, through Arafat, to Abbas, all of whom betrayed the interests and welfare of their own people on the altar of their ambition, their cupidity, and their hatred. They are severally characterized by corruption, lies, and an 'all-or-nothing' mentality. The upshot of that mentality was that they achieved nothing for their own people but more suffering. The Palestinian leaders were offered the chance of a state on numerous occasions. They refused all offers. As was wisely said by Abba Eban, they never missed an opportunity to miss an opportunity.

Ninth, western leaders, largely ignorant of the complex history and three-dimensional chessboard of Middle Eastern affairs, let alone of the mores of the Arabs, repeatedly call for ceasefires. They do not realize that among Muslims, a ceasefire, known as a *hudna*, is *doctrinally* not a prelude to peace, but no more than an opportunity over a period of ten years to regroup, rearm, and begin again. It is not surprising that the 1949 negotiations in Rhodes under the aegis of Dr Ralph Bunche for a ceasefire between Israel and its attackers in the Israel War of Independence never led to peace – the Arab states never intended them to.

Tenth, the United Nations, its committees and the General Assembly are unremittingly and remorselessly anti-Israeli and antisemitic. So too are its agencies such as UNWRA. It was indeed through UNWRA that Palestinian refugee status became, uniquely and absurdly, hereditable. The Gazans, save for a very small number who are over the age of 75, are not refugees but the children, grandchildren, or great-grandchildren of refugees.

Eleventh, while the vocal anti-Zionists and the educated classes in the West express sympathy for the Palestinian refugees from 1948, they appear to be wholly ignorant of the fact that there were significantly more Jewish refugees evicted from North Africa and the Middle East than Arab Palestinians from the Mandate. Jews from all over the Arab world were integrated into Israeli society. The Arab Palestinians were kept in Gaza and the West Bank as a showcase to demonstrate to visitors the wickedness of Israel.

This enumeration of eleven salient points will, I hope, provide a guideline for the reading of this complicated history. It will be a journey through a very complex and often ugly landscape.

Many people have encouraged me, advised me, and corrected errors in drafts of this monograph. Vernon Bogdanor's support and encyclopaedic knowledge have been invaluable. I am grateful to Tom Otte, who kindly read a late draft and suggested important corrections.

Hanoch Ben-Yami's encouragement has been heart-warming. Finally, my son Jonathan made crucial analytic suggestions and vital corrections to successive drafts as well as drafting the addenda on the Iran War when I was too unwell to do so. My son Adam and my daughter Jocelyn gave me excellent advice and rallied my spirits when I flagged.

July 17, 2025

Note

1 McMahon's double-standard argument was published in *Analyse & Kritik* 2024. A spirited reply was published by Daniel Statman in *Analyse & Kritik* 2025 (47(1)), pp. 179–207.

1   October 7, 2023

1. *The Gaza Strip and the Hamas massacre* The Gaza Strip is a small sliver of land on the eastern Mediterranean coast, bordered by Egypt in the southwest and Israel in the east and north (see Map 1). It has an area of 365 square kilometres (141 square miles). It is 41 kilometres (25 miles) long and between 6 and 12 kilometres (3.7 to 7.5 miles) wide. Its capital is Gaza City, and its second largest town is Rafah. It has a population of over 2 million, 50% of which are under the age of 18. It is populated primarily by Sunni Arabs (as opposed to Shia in Iran) with a very small number of Arab Christians. The history of the Gaza Strip will be discussed below.

On October 7, 2023, 6,000 Hamas terrorists and other terrorist groups, such as Islamic Jihad, Popular Front for the Liberation of Palestine, and Al-Aqsa Martyrs' Brigade, breached the fences separating the Gaza Strip from 21 Israeli kibbutzim, moshavim, and small townships adjacent to the strip (see Map 2).[1] A further 1,000 active terrorists remained in the Gaza Strip to keep up a constant barrage of rockets on Israeli towns and settlements further afield. 1,182 victims were slaughtered, mostly Israelis including Israeli Arabs and Bedouin, some overseas guest workers from the Philippines, Nepal, and Thailand, as well as visiting foreigners. At the Nova Music Festival that was taking place 4 kilometres from the Gaza border in the desert in the vicinity of Kibbutz Re'im, more than 370 people were killed, mostly in their 20s, many of the women being raped or gang-raped, and subsequently killed and genitally mutilated. Of the murdered victims on October 7, 863 were civilians and the remainder were soldiers. Over 4,000 were injured, some very severely. The terrorists

DOI: 10.4324/9781003711957-1

decapitated or attempted to decapitate some of the slain. They blew out the brains of babies before their parents' eyes and murdered parents in front of their children. Some mothers were strapped to their babies and burnt to death by thermobarbic grenades or explosives.[2] They threw these into homes of civilians and into safe rooms in homes in which civilians tried to barricade themselves. Many of those thus burnt to death left barely enough ashes for DNA identification. Around 251 (210 alive and 41 dead) Israelis and people of other nationality, mostly civilians, were taken hostage to be used by Hamas as bargaining chips for exchange of thousands of convicted prisoners in Israeli gaols, some serving multiple life sentences as mass murderers. This was the most atrocious slaughter of innocent, largely civilian, Jews since the Nazi Holocaust and the third deadliest terrorist attack ever.

The attacking terrorists were predominantly teenagers or in their twenties, some of whom were intoxicated with captagon (an amphetamine). They exulted in the slaughter of the innocent, especially of the attendants at the Nova Music Festival in the Negev desert. One of the terrorists, murdering Israelis at Kibbutz Mefalsim, told his parents triumphantly on his smartphone that he had killed ten Jews with his own hands, and proudly held up his bloody hands to show his mother.

2. *Hamas's ideology and funding* Hamas is an internationally condemned terrorist organization, an offshoot of the Egyptian Muslim Brotherhood. It was founded in 1987 at the commencement of the First Intifada (uprising) by Ahmed Yassin, a blind Palestinian cleric in the Gaza Strip. Its 1988 Charter called for the slaughter of Jews, the destruction of the State of Israel and the establishment of an Islamic Sharia State in 'historic Palestine'. Antisemitism is a key aspect of Hamas ideology. Articles 22–32 of its original charter use arguments derived from the *Protocols of the Elders of Zion* (see below), *Mein Kampf*, and the Ku-Klux-Klan.[3] The charter blames Jews for the French Revolution, the Russian Revolution, for both World Wars, and for the Wall Street crash of 1929. It asserts that Zionists aim to destroy society through moral corruption and elimination of Islam, drug trafficking, and alcoholism. Article 32 states that the Zionist plan is set out in the *Protocols of the Elders of Zion*. The Hamas Charter declared Hamas to be a death cult in as much as Article 8 of its constitution asserts 'Allah is its [Hamas's] goal, the Prophet is its model, the Quran its constitution, *jihad* [Holy War] its path, and death for the sake of Allah is the loftiest of its wishes.' The charter was revised in 2017, but primarily for publicity and propaganda purposes. It now asserted itself

to be enemy only of the State of Israel and of Zionism – although its genocidal intent was patent on the October 7 massacre.

Hamas was deeply involved in the First Intifada (uprising) 1987–93 and the Second Intifada 2000–2005 – neither of which was spontaneous, but was, rather, carefully planned and organized by Yasser Arafat, chairman of the Palestine Liberation Organization (PLO) from 1969 to 2004, and founding member of its militant, terrorist wing Fatah. In the course of the Intifadas, Hamas, in the Gaza Strip, claimed responsibility for 20 suicide bombings in Israel, killing 187 people and injuring 1,150.

In 2005, local elections were held in the Palestinian Authority's territory, including the Gaza Strip. Hamas won seven of the ten councils. In the 2006 elections the Hamas alliance Change and Reform won 44.5% of the vote to Fatah's 42% but won an overwhelming majority of the seats. As a result, Ismael Haniyeh (1962–2024) became Prime Minister of the Palestinian Authority as a whole, an office that the Bush administration pushed for in order to sideline Arafat. A power struggle between Haniyeh and Mahmoud Abbas ensued over who controlled the security services in the Palestinian territories. This turned deadly in 2007, when Fatah crushed Hamas in the West Bank, while Hamas murdered the Fatah officials in the Gaza Strip, throwing them off high-rise buildings, shooting them in the back, or tying them face down behind motorcycles and dragging them along until they were dead. Abbas formed an emergency government with a new prime minister on the West Bank and the political divide between the Palestinian Authority and the Gaza Strip was sealed.

Haniyah was the Hamas leader in the Gaza Strip from June 2007 until February 2017, when he was elected chairman of the Hamas Political Bureau (replacing Khaled Mashal) in Qatar. He lived there (in great luxury) until his assassination by Mossad in 2024. The Hamas leadership, like the leadership of the PLO, which will be examined below, was for the most part deeply corrupt, and siphoned off large sums of money for their own use. Khaled Mashal and Haniyah alike were said to be in possession of $4 billion each. The leader of Hamas in the Gaza Strip was Yahya Sinwar (1962–2024), who succeeded Haniyah as leader in the Gaza Strip in 2017. Sinwar (who was not financially corrupt), was sentenced in Israel to four life sentences in 1989 for murdering two Israeli soldiers and four Palestinians who were accused of collaboration with Israeli authorities. He spent 22 years in Israeli prison and was released in 2011, in a prisoner exchange for Gilad Shalit, an Israeli corporal kidnapped by Hamas.

To obtain Shalit's freedom Israel released more than 1,000 convicted prisoners conjunctively responsible for 569 deaths of Israelis. Sinwar, whose life had been saved in an Israeli hospital from death from a brain tumour, was sworn to the total destruction of Israel. 'When you are weak', he said to an Israeli doctor, 'we'll tear your hearts out'.

In recent years, Hamas has been funded primarily by Qatar[4] and Iran,[5] and, often inadvertently, by the USA,[6] the European Union (EU),[7] the UK,[8] and the UN.[9] It has international investments of £500 million in real estate in Algeria, Saudi Arabia, Sudan, Turkey, and UAE.[10] International food aid was used by Hamas for political purposes. It controlled and taxed food supplies in the Strip, rewarding the families of its supporters and recruits, and extorting the compliance of all others. Despite occasional public statements that Hamas's aim is only the destruction of the State of Israel ('the Zionist entity' as they call it), it is clear that Hamas is explicitly committed to the slaughter of the Jewish population of the State of Israel. Article 7 of their 1988 Charter quotes from a hadith (a purported saying of Mohammed):

> The Day of Judgement will not come until Muslims fight the Jews, when the Jews will hide behind stones and trees. The stones and trees will say 'O Muslim, O servant of God, there is a Jew behind me. Come and kill him.'

Hamas's spokesman, Ghazi Hamad, speaking on Lebanon's LBC TV on October 24, 2023, said: 'Everything we do is justified', adding 'The al Aqsa Flood [Hamas's name for their onslaught] is just the first time, and there will be a second, a third, a fourth because we have the determination, the resolve, and the capabilities to fight.' It would be difficult to be clearer than that.

3. *Israel caught by surprise* The Israeli government, the Israel Defence Forces (IDF), the Israeli Intelligence Services (Mossad), and the Internal Security Service (Shabak) were caught unawares on October 7, 2023, in much the same way as they had been 50 years earlier in the 1973 Yom Kippur War. Their inattention was largely due to (a) complacency; (b) inadequacies in the operation and coordination of Shabak, Mossad, and the IDF; and (c) Netanyahu's personal responsibility, as yet not subjected to post-bellum judicial investigation.

(a) The prime minister, Benjamin Netanyahu, as the head of the most conservative and reactionary government in the history of the State, had allowed billions of dollars to be funnelled into Hamas's hands by Qatar and Iran (over and above the billions of dollars donated by the UN, the USA, and the EU). He believed, like many, that allowing money to flow into Gaza from Qatar and other sources, would give ordinary Gazans a better standard of living. In turn, this would foster an interest in not risking an all-out war. That turned out to be a disastrous misjudgement. In fact, the money was used largely to purchase weapons, produce tens of thousands of missiles and to build a multi-level reinforced concrete network of tunnels. This was, to be sure, known by Israel from the previous Gazan wars in response to Hamas's persistent rocket-firing onto the adjacent Israeli towns and villages, but no one appears to have realized the extent and thoroughness of this underground pre-prepared battlefield. These tunnels are more than 400 miles long and five levels deep.[11] That is more extensive and deeper than the London Underground. The government of Israel held that an attitude of periodic crisis management was adequate. This betokened an unwarranted complacency on behalf of the government as a background circumstance of the disaster. Israel was altogether unprepared, intellectually and militarily, for a major assault from Hamas and a prolonged war.

(b) The Internal Security Services and the IDF under the command of Lieutenant General Herzi Halevi, as well as the head of Southern Command, Major General Yaron Finkelman, and the Head of the Military Intelligence Directorate, Major General Aharon Haliva, were lax in both the gathering of information on Hamas and its plans, and the interpretation of the signs that were available. Israel intelligence gathering in Gaza was less comprehensive than in the West Bank. There was an assumption that the threat posed by Hezbollah, under direct control of Iran, and armed with 150,000 missiles directed at Israeli cities, towns, and villages, posed a greater clear and present danger to Israel than Hamas in Gaza. They all subsequently admitted responsibility for their failings and resigned once the major fighting was over and a ceasefire implemented.

(c) The final factor to be considered is Netanyahu's personal responsibility, since these events happened on his watch. Netanyahu has thus far resisted pressure to form an independent judicial Commission of Enquiry into the Gaza War on the model of the post-1973 Yom Kippur War Commission of Enquiry. This can be justified on the grounds that the war is still not over – the 1973

Commission was set up after the end of the war. But it may also raise suspicion that he is trying to cover up his own culpability.[12] Be that as it may, as things stand, one cannot say more than that he shared the same assumptions as the IDF – that Gaza's problems were containable and contained.

4. *Hezbollah: Iran's proxy* By its attack on October 7, Hamas had begun a war. Hamas hoped that Hezbollah, under the leadership of Hassan Nasrallah and deeply entrenched in Lebanon, would attack Israel in the north in the same way as soon as they heard of the Hamas onslaught. The plan worked out by the Iranian Revolutionary Guard was for simultaneous attack in both northern Israel from Hezbollah and southern Israel from Hamas. However, Hamas did not notify Hezbollah of the date of its attack, being afraid that any communication would be intercepted by Israeli intelligence services. Hezbollah was, therefore, caught by surprise.

Hezbollah was a direct proxy of the Iranian theocratic dictatorship, who, more than a 1,000 miles away and with no territorial conflict with Israel, was sworn to the eradication of the State of Israel and to the slaughter of its Jewish citizens. The first Supreme Leader of Iran, after the Iranian revolution of 1979, Ayatollah Khomeini, had decreed that America was the Great Satan, while Israel was the Little Satan. His successor as ruler of Iran since 1989, Ayatollah Khamenei, continues to refer to Israel as a cancer in the Middle East, to call for and to plot its annihilation. Incitement to genocide, a constant refrain of the Iranian theocratic regime and of Iranian military leaders, is a crime in international law.

Hezbollah, like its Iranian masters, was of the Shia persuasion (unlike Hamas). It was trained, funded, and closely advised by senior commanders of the Revolutionary Guard of the Iranian regime. It was in effect a state within a state and had dominating representation in the Lebanese government.

Hamas and Hezbollah between them, with the support of Iran and its proxies, the Houthi rebels in Yemen hoped to destroy the State of Israel or at any rate bring about a pan-Middle Eastern war and undermine the Abraham Accords initiated by Donald Trump in 2020, during his first administration. The Abraham Accords were bilateral agreements between Israel and the UAE in the Persian Gulf, between Israel and Bahrain in the Persian Gulf, and between Israel and Morocco, in all of which Israel's sovereignty was recognized.

The Abraham Accords were designed to normalize relations and to facilitate commerce and tourism between the signatories. Hamas, as well as the Iranians and their proxies Hezbollah, were fearful that the Abraham Accords would signal the beginning of peaceful relations in the Middle East and bypass the Palestinian cause, on the one hand, and stymie Iranian regional power dominance, on the other.

In the event, Hezbollah did not invade Israel, but rather bombarded the north of Israel with missiles, causing the evacuation of approximately 100,000 Israeli citizens from their homes for over a year,[13] destroying numerous buildings, agricultural lands, and causing extensive forest fires.

When Israel, after a year of intense warfare, did finally attack Hezbollah in the north, it became clear that the underground tunnels Hezbollah had built along the Lebanese/Israel border were prepared for an analogous attack from the north which would similarly slaughter countless Jews and take civilian hostages. Hezbollah had taken over the whole of southern Lebanon and south Beirut. Virtually every house had been transformed into a rocket launching base, with owners of the houses being forced to accept the transformation and given payment for it (see Map 3).

5. *Existential war on 7 fronts* From October 7, 2023, Israel found itself fighting an existential war for its very survival on seven fronts: Gaza (Hamas), Lebanon (Hezbollah), Syria (Asad), Yemen (Houthis), Judaea and Samaria[14] (where the PLO, PFLP, and Islamic Jihad were deeply embedded in the so-called refugee camps[15] in Jenin and Nablus), Iraq, and Iran. Iran fought a proxy war against Israel for much of the time. But it became actively engaged in firing hundreds of ballistic missiles and drones at Israel in April and again in October 2024, most of which were successfully intercepted by Israel's sophisticated defence systems and the American naval task force in the area.

6. *Israel the sole democracy in the Middle East: siding against Israel is a transformation of antisemitism* Israel is the only democracy in the whole of the Middle East and North Africa. There is universal suffrage – Israeli Arabs have representatives in the Knesset and have their own parties as well as members in other parties. They have at times been in the government. Israeli Arabs have been ambassadors in the Israeli foreign service. That said, its Arab population is the poorest segment of society and under the current government, its financial support has been further cut. Policing in the Arab towns and villages is inadequate,

and locally elected Arab village and town councils are notoriously corrupt. Israel has a free press (including Arab newspapers), an independent judiciary (with Israeli Arab representation on the judiciary; Israeli Arabs have had a judge on the Israeli Supreme Court). Israel allows freedom of religion, universal access to education – primary, secondary, and tertiary. It has a well-developed national health system accessible to all, as well as child allowances, unemployment benefits and retirement pensions. Its Jewish population is over 7 million, its Arab population is 2 million (Muslim 1.86 million and Christian 0.14 million). Its per capita GDP is equal to that of the UK.

Against this background, one might have expected the Western world of representative democracies to rally to Israel's side and to give it full support in its war against Hamas, Hezbollah, Syria, Iran, the Houthis, occasionally the Iraqis, and the terrorist groups embedded in the West Bank. One might have supposed the educated classes, universities, and university students to demonstrate their abhorrence and to support Israel's existential seven-front war. That, however, was not what happened. One of the purposes of this essay is to explain why so many progressive left-wingers all over the Western world should have self-righteously aligned themselves with genocidal terrorists against the only liberal democracy in the Middle East. Criticism of Israel and of the Israeli government is one thing, at which many Israelis, Israeli newspapers and broadcasters excel. That is not antisemitism. Supporting Hamas, Hezbollah, the Houthis, and Iran in their quest to destroy Israel is another. Anti-Zionism denies the right of the State of Israel to exist. That *is* a form of antisemitism.

Notes

1 Figures taken from the British *7th October Parliamentary Commission Report Chaired by Lord Roberts of Belgravia*, which contains the most exhaustive and reliable report on the horrors of October 7.
2 Thermobarbic grenades and explosives burn at a temperature of 3,000 degrees centigrade. Terrorists tossed them into homes of the villagers in the kibbutzim and moshavim around the Gaza Strip.
3 See *7th October Parliamentary Commission Report Chaired by Lord Roberts of Belgravia*, p. 27.
4 Between 2012 and 2020, Qatar donated $1.3 billion to the Gaza Strip. Most of this ended up in the hands of Hamas.
5 According to US Department of Treasury and Secretary of State Blinken in the administration of President Biden.

6 USAID has contributed $2.1 billion in aid for Gaza since October 7, 2023, 90% of which ended up in Hamas-controlled areas. This in effect enabled Hamas to survive until the ceasefire in January/February 2025 (see evidence of Greg Roman, executive director of Middle East Forum to the Sub-Committee on Delivering Government Efficiency, February 2025).

7 The EU paid over €100 million to UNWRA (the UN Relief and Works Agency for Palestine) in 2023, €82 million in 2024, and €120 million in 2025, despite the fact that UNWRA in the Gaza Strip is in effect a branch of Hamas, many of its staff are also members of Hamas, and it has been in control of antisemitic education and antisemitic schoolbooks in the Gaza Strip and in the refugee camps (cities) of the so-called West Bank (Judaea and Samaria) for decades. See Chapter 6, Section 4.

8 The UK government contributed over £100 million to Palestine Authority and Gaza in 2023/4, which included £10 million to the Palestinian Authority to pay public sector salaries and UNICEF, and £34 million for UNWRA. Half of this was delivered through UNWRA. How it was used merits investigation.

9 According to Associated Press, between 2014 and 2020 UN agencies spent nearly $4.5 billion in Gaza, 80% of which was channelled through UNWRA.

10 According to the US Department of Treasury.

11 According to John Spencer, chair of Urban Warfare Studies at West Point, New York (interview, March 31, 2025).

12 Netanyahu's policies have, for many years, been devious and eminently challengeable. When the Palestine Authority was seen as the major threat, he connived at funds reaching Hamas to strengthen their standing, in the hope that this would reduce the international plausibility of the leadership of the Palestine Authority (see Jonathan Meta 'Qatargate lays bare Israel's gamble on Hamas rule', *Times of Israel* blog, April 5, 2025).

13 Figure of evacuees from B. Ben-Muvhar, Head of Mevo'ot HaHermon Regional Council.

14 Judaea and Samaria are in effect what *was* called the 'West Bank' of the Hashemite Kingdom of Jordan. It had been part of the British Mandate of Palestine. It was conquered by King Abdullah's Arab Legion (armed and officered by British troops under the command of Sir John Glubb Pasha) in Israel's War of Independence in 1948. It was retaken by Israel in the Six-Day War of 1967 after King Husain of Jordan, having been warned by Israel to keep out of the war which Egypt had initiated, was cajoled into joining Nasser of Egypt and Nureddin al-Atassi of Syria. Since the Oslo agreements, the West Bank has been divided into segments, some under direct control of the Palestinian Authority, led by Mahmoud Abbas, some under direct Israeli rule. Israel has permitted some areas to be settled by approximately half a million Jewish settlers. This has been a disastrous policy. Many of the settlers are fanatics and inflict much harm – physical,

financial, and moral, on the Arab Palestinians around them, who in turn engage in extensive terror attacks against Israeli settlers. The Israeli Internal Security Services (Shabak) all too often turn a blind eye to the criminal behaviour of the settlers. The Palestinians engage in terror attacks against the Israeli settlers and also in attacks inside the 'Green line' (the armistice line of 1949), where they stab, shoot, or use cars to run over Israelis. In Nablus and Jenin in particular, Hamas and Islamic Jihad have well-established cells supported and advised by Iran. It is one of the Iranian principles in their struggle to annihilate Israel that Israel will be destroyed on the West Bank. The deadly terrorism and counter-terrorism constitute a grievous and interminable cycle of violence (in *some* respects akin to the Northern Ireland conflict that beset the UK for so many decades).

15 'So-called' in as much as they are not camps and do not consist of tents but are poorly built cities made of concrete and stone.

2 Anti-Zionism

1. *Hamas's underground fortifications; use of hospitals, schools, mosques* Once the IDF had gathered its wits together, it began to respond to the incessant barrage of thousands of rockets from Gaza directed at Israeli cities, towns, and agricultural settlements and intended to kill as many civilians as possible. As already noted, the Hamas terrorists had had nineteen years to build a unique underground city specifically designed for insurgency urban warfare. Nothing like this has existed in the world (although there are some parallels with the underground supply routes built by the Vietcong in the Vietnam War).

The home-made rockets of Hamas and Islamic Jihad in Gaza (unlike the missiles sent to Hezbollah from Iran via Syria) were made from pipes given by the EU and other donor nations to create a water supply and sewerage system in Gaza. The machinery to convert pipes to rockets was smuggled into Gaza through the Egyptian controlled Sinai desert, perhaps through the bribery of Egyptian officers tempted by a large Swiss or London bank account. The tunnels on the Egyptian side of the Rafah border were wide enough for two trucks to drive through side by side. They were within sight of an observation post of the Egyptian army, who made no attempt to stop the illegal transport of goods to Hamas (despite its being an internationally recognized terrorist organization).

The Hamas terrorists had mined and booby-trapped countless houses in the Strip, kept weapons (and hostages) in hospitals, and had built the tunnels from which they could fire RPGs (rocket-propelled grenades) and batteries of rockets next to schools, mosques, and United Nations agencies. This is a war crime. They were therefore deliberately using such institutions and the civilians who took refuge from danger in them, as human shields. This too is a war crime. They

DOI: 10.4324/9781003711957-2

knew full-well that any civilian casualties consequent upon Israeli attacks on Hamas firing positions and weapon-stores would result in civilian casualties that would further their cause in the arena of public opinion around the world and in international reactions to the war. This too is contrary to international law. As far as Hamas was concerned, the more Gazan casualties the better.

This forced the IDF to fight an unprecedently difficult and dangerous form of urban warfare. It has sometimes been compared to the allied war in Iraq against the extreme terrorist group ISIS/ISIL (Islamic State in Syria/Islamic State in the Levant – two different names for the same organization) in Mosul and Raqqa in 2017. However, they are altogether incomparable wars. The ISIL defenders had not had two decades to prepare the urban terrain for warfare. There was no underground system of tunnels on five different levels. The allied war against ISIL was traditional, brutal, urban, counter-insurgency warfare. Consequently, civilian casualty figures, probably much higher in Mosul and Raqqa than in the Gaza War, are not really comparable.[1]

There were, to be sure, civilian casualties including innocent preteen children, whose suffering was appalling. The numbers of civilian casualties were, however, not remotely as great as were reported by Hamas's spokesmen or by UNWRA officials.

2. *Corruption of UNWRA* UNWRA, the United Nations Relief and Works Agency for Palestinian Refugees in the Near East was set up in 1949 to provide aid to 700,000 Palestinian refugees after the Israeli War of Independence (this figure is almost certainly exaggerated (see Chapter VI, fn. 3)). Unique among world refugees, Palestinian refugee status is hereditable: children, grandchildren, and great-grandchildren of 1948 refugees count as refugees. That is logically incoherent – but logic is of little moment in the matter. There are now (2025) 5.9 million Palestinian refugees, 2 million in the Gaza Strip. UNWRA is the largest of all UN agencies, employing over 30,000 staff, 99% locally recruited Palestinians. Its annual income is approximately one billion dollars. In the course of the war, UNWRA was discovered to be extensively infiltrated by Hamas. The educational system for which it was responsible was explicitly antisemitic and *jihadist*. This will be discussed below.

3. *Hamas's falsification of casualty figures* Hamas reports of children killed or injured follow the UNWRA custom of counting anyone up to the age of eighteen as a child entitled to free food and education.

A large proportion of the Hamas terrorists were teenagers, hence described as children when killed or injured. Hamas's announced figures of Gazans killed by Israelis included not only such 'children', but also natural deaths in the Strip over the period of the war. These falsified figures were repeated and indeed given priority throughout the Western press, radio and TV stations.

4. *Israel strives to minimize collateral damage* The ratio of civilian deaths to combatant deaths (known as 'collateral damage') appears to have been 1:1.1, lower than in any comparable counter-insurgency war in the history of warfare.[2] Israel took more measures to minimize collateral damage than any other army in comparable forms of war, announcing to Gazans by leaflets and by millions of telephone calls when and where they were going to bomb and instructing the Gazan non-combatants which areas would be safe. Inevitably, the buildings of Gaza were reduced to rubble. The consequences of counter-insurgency urban warfare for civilians, both in terms of casualties and homelessness are dreadful.

5. *International responses: demonization of Israel* The response to the Gaza War in the months after October 7, 2023, was not merely criticism of Israel, justified or unjustified as the case may be. It was denominated 'anti-Zionism', which is, at first glance, distinct from anti-semitism. Anti-Zionism denies the right of Israel to exist. But the Jews have a right to a state of their own, a right recognized by the League of Nations, by the 1922 establishment of the British Mandate to be a national home for the Jews, and by the United Nations in 1947. The accusations levelled at Israel under the novel guise of 'anti-Zionism' were patently antisemitic. Anti-Zionism spread across the whole of the Western world, Europe and North America, as well as the antipodean lands of Australia and New Zealand. The South African government also joined the fray in the International Court of Justice (ICJ) and the International Criminal Court (ICC). Israel was accused of genocide; neo-colonialism; apartheid; racialism; violations of international law; collective punishment of the Gazans; and the indiscriminate murder of children. This gross, indeed grotesque, inversion of the truth was reminiscent of medieval blood libels and consequent slaughter of Jews. Every offense of which Israel was accused was in fact, as will be shown, committed by Hamas, Hezbollah, and the Arab states supporting them. The Gaza War became akin to a Dreyfus Case of the 2020s, in as much as it divided society and families alike in a comparable manner. To

be sure, Dreyfus was wholly innocent of any misdemeanour, whereas Israel was not. But that does not distinguish it from any other states in the world, all of whom opt for Realpolitik when pushed.

6. *Anti-Zionism is a transmutation of antisemitism* Anti-Zionism was manifested on the streets within weeks of October 7. Demonstrations of hundreds of thousands of people poured through the capital cities of Europe, USA, Canada, and Australia for weekend after weekend, shouting such slogans as 'From the river to the sea, Palestine will be free', which calls for the destruction of the State of Israel, if not also for the slaughter of its citizens.[3] Large proportions of these crowds were Muslims showing solidarity with Gazans and with Hamas; many others were simply left-wing sympathizers with similar sympathies with the Hamas mass murderers. These demonstrations were anything but spontaneous. They were carefully organized and funded by pro-Palestinian organizations (in Britain by The Palestine Solidarity Campaign, the chief proponent of BDS (Boycott, Divest, and Sanction) and of anti-Israeli accusations of apartheid).

7. *Biden's equivocal support of Israel* There was initial support for Israel's plight from some Western governments and explicit vocal support from President Biden in the USA. He immediately responded to the October 7 massacres by characterizing them as 'pure evil' and he allowed the delivery of arms and munitions to Israel.

Nevertheless, Biden's support was decidedly equivocal, not out of ill will, but out of ignorance and misunderstanding. As the war wore on, Biden's mental powers patently wore out. He sought to micromanage the IDF and IAF bombing operations without any understanding of the military situation or of the Hamas and Hezbollah mentality. He stopped the IAF from attacking Teheran's nuclear program and centrifuge production facilities for weapon-grade uranium, forbade the IAF from attacking Iran's oil facilities. He blocked delivery of 2,000 lb. MK-84 bombs despite Congressional approval, and he slowed down delivery of MK-83 and MK-82 bombs and the Joint Direct Attack Munition kits that convert these bombs into guided munitions. The State Department stalled delivery of thousands of Hellfire missiles, tank and mortar shells, as well as more than 100 armoured bulldozers that aid infantry attacking booby-trapped buildings. Supply shortages reduced IAF bombing of Hezbollah targets in Lebanon from 3,000 per day to 1,000. He tried to stop, and succeeded in long delaying, Israel's incursion into Rafah – a delay which prolonged the war.

8. *Cease-fire and Islamic doctrine of 'hudna'* Virtually all Western leaders maintained a constant call for a ceasefire – most prominently Biden's secretary of state Anthony Blinken who was tireless in his attempts to emulate Henry Kissinger's shuttle diplomacy in 1973–5, pleading futilely for a ceasefire on all fronts and for the return of hostages taken by Hamas.

Few, if any, western leaders seemed able to grasp the simple fact that a ceasefire would play into the hands of Iran and its proxies, Hamas and Hezbollah, who would seize upon a ceasefire in order to regroup and rearm in accordance with the advice given to the faithful by the Islamic doctrine of *hudna* – a ceasefire is not a prelude to peace negotiations, but a pragmatic military move of *reculer pour mieux sauter*. It should have been no surprise after 1949, when, in the name of the United Nations, Dr Ralph Bunche negotiated the ceasefire in Rhodes after the Israeli War of Independence, that what had never been intended as permanent borders became ossified. No Arab state that had assailed Israel meant the ceasefire to be anything other than a *hudna*. But now, Western nations and Western liberal thinkers assign to the so-called 'green line' a permanence that it was never meant to have, since it left Israel a mere 10 miles wide between Netanya and Tulkarm.

9. *International leaders* President Macron of France was prominent in his castigation of Israel, constantly calling for ceasefires on the northern, Lebanese front. It is unclear what motivated him. France had had a long association with Lebanon since the First World War, and it had exceedingly lucrative investments with Lebanon to rebuild Beirut Harbour and its environs that were blown to pieces in the explosion of huge quantities of ammonium nitrate on August 4, 2020. There were 218 fatalities, 7,000 injured, 300,000 displaced persons, and $15 billion damage to property. Hezbollah's involvement in the purchase, storage, and use of the chemical for production of explosives was suspected but never proved (or disproved) – although it is noteworthy that Hezbollah leaders in Lebanon opposed the publication of any investigations into the explosion. Macron obtained the lucrative contract for reconstruction for French companies. It is not known what, if any, agreements with Hezbollah were involved in the granting of the contract. Macron is now intent on granting Mahmoud Abbas recognition of Palestine as a state. It is by no means clear what that means, since the Palestinians on the West Bank do not legally constitute a state and French recognition does not make it one. But whatever

Macron means by this, it is a signal to Abbas and the terrorist groups in the West Bank, that terrorism pays and gets rewarded.

The Irish President, Michael Higgins castigated talk of anti-semitism in Ireland as 'a PR exercise'. He criticized Israel for having quoted a private congratulatory letter he wrote to the newly elected president of Iran Masoud Pezeshkian (not to be confused with the Supreme Leader), expressing his condolences for the death in a plane crash of the previous Iranian President Ebrahim Raisi, also known as the 'butcher of Iran' for the murders he committed when Ayatollah Khomeni seized power in Iran.[4] The contents of the letter were publicly available on Iranian websites and there was nothing private about it any longer. President Higgins was singularly vocal in his unqualified condemnation of Israel's conduct of the seven-front war, choosing to do so – of all times – on Holocaust Day. Israel found this unacceptable and withdrew its ambassador from Ireland.[5]

The British foreign secretary David Lammy, after visiting Israel and the Palestinian authority territories, was adamant in calling for a ceasefire and for an immediate two-state solution – without pausing to think what exactly a two-state solution would be. This 'solution', constantly advanced by Western politicians, will be examined below. Lammy also threatened to cease supplying Israel with weapons, in particular essential spare parts for its fighter aircraft that are manufactured under licence from the USA. This was not actually done, perhaps partly because that would violate contractual agreements with the Americans, partly because Israel would, presumably, purchase the spare parts directly from the USA, and partly because Britain buys more high-tech military equipment for its own armed forces from Israel than Israel buys military supplies from Britain.

The Australian prime minister Anthony Albanese was vociferous in calling for an Israeli-ceasefire as was Justin Trudeau in Canada.

10. *UN: Guterres' bigotry, UN general assembly and F. Albanese's antisemitism* The UN had, for many years, been indiscriminately and continuously critical of the State of Israel. Following October 7, 2023, it acted true to form. Secretary General Antonio Guterres[6] rarely missed an opportunity to condemn Israel. He asserted that Hamas's attack 'did not happen in a vacuum' and that 'the Palestinian people have been subjected to 56 years of suffocating occupation'[7] – disregarding the fact that the Palestinian leaders had been offered a state by three successive Israeli prime ministers and turned it down on

each occasion.[8] The Arab Palestinians, ever since Amin Husseini in the 1920s, have been lamentably ill-served by their leaders.

Between 2015 and the end of 2022, the UN General Assembly adopted 140 resolutions condemning Israel, by contrast with 68 resolutions against the whole of the rest of the world. Between 2006 and 2022 the UN Human Rights Council adopted 99 resolutions against Israel, more than against the whole of the rest of the world (including Russia, China, Iraq, Iran, Venezuela, Sudan, Somalia, etc.). Guterres recurrently mooted the possibility or probability that Israel was committing genocide and crimes against humanity in Gaza. These accusations, as will be argued below, were groundless. It was Hamas and Hezbollah that were explicitly committed to, and committed, genocide and crimes against humanity. Franceska Albanese, the UN Special Rapporteur on human rights in the 'Palestinian territories' is an Italian lawyer with a savage hatred of Israel and Jews in general. In 2015 she compared the so-called 'Nakba' to the Nazi Holocaust.[9] To be sure, she did not indicate in what respects the Palestinian refugees are victims of a holocaust, especially since their numbers have grown, in Gaza alone, from 200,000 in 1948 to 2 million today. She inveighs against the 'Jewish Lobby' in the USA, as if the Jews are the only group in the USA to lobby congress – generally repeating doctrines of the 'Protocols of the Elders of Zion'[10] that the Jews control the world. She compared the Israelis to Nazis, expressed sympathy with terrorist organizations such as Hamas, accused Israel of war crimes, referred to Israel as a 'settler-colonial enterprise' and to Jews in Israel as 'foreign interlopers'. She was reappointed to her post in April 2025. Miloon Kothari, a member of the UN's commission of enquiry into alleged Israeli war crimes pronounced (in conformity with the Protocols of the Elders of Zion) that social media are 'controlled largely by the Jewish Lobby' and questioned why Israel was allowed into the UN at all.

11. *Jeremy Bowen and BBC's pro-Hamas propaganda* Broadcasting services tended to be equally anti-Israeli throughout the West. The BBC was particularly egregious on its radio and television services in the UK and on its much-respected overseas services with audiences of hundreds of millions. It adamantly refused to refer to Hamas as a terrorist organization or to Hamas operatives as terrorists but was liberal in referring currently to Jewish terrorism in 1947 (when the King David hotel was blown up by the Irgun, who gave a 20-minute

warning), and in referring to Itamar Ben-Gvir as a supporter of Jewish terrorism and inciter of racism. The BBC persisted in asking whether Israel could not stop the bombing of Gaza, but it seems not to have occurred to its editors and broadcasters to ask whether Hamas could not stop firing rockets and RPGs and return the hostages they had taken. It is worth briefly describing the lengths to which it went in its anti-Israeli propaganda under the aegis of Jeremy Bowen.

Bowen was the BBC Middle East correspondent based in Jerusalem from 1995 to 2000, BBC Middle East editor from 2005 until 2022, when he became the international editor of BBC news. It was in May 2000 that he, with a friend, covering the Israeli withdrawal from Lebanon, was caught in crossfire in which his friend and colleague was killed. Unsurprisingly, any impartiality thereafter could hardly be expected and arguably he should have recused himself or been recused from broadcasting on Israeli affairs. Nevertheless, he has been in control of BBC Middle East reporting for many years and, presumably, involved in appointments and in directing. So it was he who hired or instructed the hiring of Gazans to report events in Gaza during the war, knowing full well that most of them could not say a word without the approval of Hamas and that at least some of them were on the Hamas payroll. It was under his tutelage that Hamas figures for casualties were identified as such and juxtaposed with IDF evidence as if the two were on a par, knowing perfectly well that the figures given by Hamas were announced for purely pragmatic considerations of propaganda advantage and with no concern whatsoever for truth. Whenever he could, Bowen cast aspersions on Israel and the IDF, all the while striking a dignified pose of neutrality. This was most strikingly revealed in his report on the alleged bombing of the Al Ahli Gazan hospital on October 17, 2023. What actually happened was that a stray rocket fired by Islamic Jihad hit the carpark of the hospital causing tens of casualties. Bowen himself reported that Israel had deliberately flattened the hospital, causing hundreds of casualties. Jon Donnison, on the BBC 10 pm news that day, announced that 500 people had been killed and then the reporter in Gaza said 'It is hard to see what else this could be – given the size of the explosion, other than an Israeli airstrike or several airstrikes'. This was the allegation made by the Gaza Health Ministry. When the truth of the matter was revealed by American satellite observations issued by the State Department, Bowen shrugged his shoulders, saying, 'Oh well, I got that one wrong didn't I?' In Parliament, the Prime Minister

Rishi Sunak warned that statements from Hamas had as much credibility as statements from the Kremlin. The BBC false reporting had serious consequences: it set off anti-Israeli rioting across the Middle East and further, and it persuaded Mahmoud Abbas not to meet President Biden for discussions.

On November 15, 2023, Israeli troops entered the Shifa Hospital in search of Hamas terrorists and Israeli hostages. The BBC news presenter asserted that the Israelis were 'targeting medical teams and Arab speakers'. It did not report that the Israeli army spokesman had said that the troops were accompanied by Arab speakers and medical teams to assist the removal of patients from danger. Later, Jeremy Bowen dismissed the significance of Kalashnikov rifles found in the hospital, arguing that perhaps they belonged to internal security hospital staff, since 'wherever you go in the Middle East you see an awful lot of Kalashnikovs'. As a dear friend of mine is fond of saying, that would be funny, if it were funny.

The BBC violated its own code of impartial reporting at least fifteen hundred times in less than a year.[11] The BBC Middle Eastern Arabic services have come in for particular criticism, portraying Israel not so much as a state to be criticized as a subject for mockery and delegitimization. More recently (February 2025) the BBC screened a programme about life in Gaza for an ordinary fourteen-year-old boy and three other children. The boy turned out to be Abdullah al-Yazouri, the son of a leading Hamas apparatchik, Ayman al-Yazouri, deputy minister of agriculture in the Gaza Strip. The commentary was systematically and deliberately mistranslated by the BBC English broadcast in the UK – every mention of the Jews and of *jihad* (holy war) being translated as 'the Israelis' and 'resistance' or 'fighting'. The BBC paid £400,000 for this film, some of which presumably was paid directly or indirectly to Hamas.

12. *Bias of left-wing press, anti-Zionism in universities* Distinguished newspapers in the anglophone world were no different, especially the left of centre press, such as *The Guardian* and *The Independent* in Britain, *The Washington Post* and *The New York Times* in the USA. Anti-Zionism was widespread in universities,[12] among academics and students, gaining very much more support from left-wing people under the age of thirty than from traditional right-wing neo-fascists and neo-Nazis. Hundreds of university departments and tens of thousands of university students throughout the West became

obsessed with the Gaza war, furiously yelling anti-Zionist slogans, advocating the destruction of the State of Israel, openly siding with Hamas. Israeli students were ostracized, humiliated, discriminated against, and sometimes physically assaulted in the USA in Columbia University, Harvard, Princeton, Berkeley, Pittsburgh, University of Michigan at Ann Arbour, DePaul University in Chicago, Brown University, and others. The same behaviour was manifested in the UK, throughout the European Union, as well as in Norway, Sweden, and Switzerland. Jewish lecturers were often prevented from lecturing and got no support from their university authorities, who claimed that genocidal howls of execration were free speech. The better educated people were and the more they conceived of themselves to be 'progressive', the more likely they were to be participating in antisemitic demonstrations. Students were shouting for another intifada, without knowing what 'intifada' meant or amounted to as long as it meant the destruction of the State of Israel. They yelled the slogan 'From the river to the sea' without even knowing which river and what sea – but knowing that it implied the slaughter of Israeli Jews.

In the Spring semester 2024, an opinion poll was conducted on sixty different US campuses in universities with large Jewish student bodies. The results help to put the student phenomenon into perspective. The resulting multivariate statistical analyses found that non-Jewish students fell into four groups with regard to their attitudes towards Israel and towards Jews. 66% of non-Jewish students displayed no hostility to Jews or to the existence of the State of Israel, although they may have disagreed with Israel's policies in Gaza. 15% of non-Jewish students were extremely hostile towards Israel. They felt that Israel had no right to exist. They did not want to associate with anyone who did believe Israel has a right to exist, so they in effect ostracized nearly all of their Jewish peers. These students were found almost exclusively on the political left. Their criticism of Israel and support for 'decolonialization' were in line with their political orientation. 16% of non-Jewish students endorsed at least one antisemitic stereotype (e.g. 'Jews have too much power in America', 'Supporters of Israel control the media'). 2% of non-Jewish students were extremely hostile to Jews and to Israel. Among the conclusions of the survey was that colleges and universities need to recognize that there is a minority of students who are contributing to a hostile environment for Jewish students on campuses.[13] This social phenomenon, not only in the USA but also in Canada, the UK, Continental Europe, and the antipodes needs explanation, which, unsurprisingly, will be multifactoral. Anti-Zionism was, in effect, a *novel* form of antisemitism – namely: left-wing neo-Marxist antisemitism. To explain this requires a brief historical digression to explain the metamorphosis of antisemitism throughout the ages.

Notes

1 See John Spencer, chair of Urban Warfare Studies at West Point, New York (interview 31 March, 2025).

2 See various depositions by British Colonel Richard Kemp (who had fought in the British army in Iraq and Afghanistan) to the UN and to the UK government. The ratio in the Allied war on ISIL in Mosul and Raqqa has been variously estimated as between 1:5 and 1:9. According to the UN the global average in urban warfare is 1:9. The USA and British average in the Iraq War was asserted to be 1:3 and in Afghanistan 1:5. All these figures are guesstimates and, in a sense, are irrelevant to the issues under debate. Collateral damage in warfare is, according to international law, 'proportional' and not contrary to international law, as long as it does not exceed what is necessary for the achievement of the military objective pursued and involves no gratuitous slaughter of civilians or troops that have surrendered. The definition of 'combatant' encompasses not merely fighters, but also anyone who harbours a hostage. Consequently, heads of hospitals or hospital departments who allowed hostages to be held on the premises of their hospitals qualify as combatants.

3 Strikingly, that slogan was illegal in Berlin and Vienna.

4 This was reminiscent of Eamon de Valera's calling on the German Minister in Dublin on May 2, 1945 to offer his condolences on Hitler's death. This may have accorded with diplomatic protocol, but it was of questionable moral propriety.

5 There are only 2,500 Jews in Ireland out of a population of more than 4.5 million, i.e. 0.55%. Nevertheless, antisemitic sentiment abounds: 49% think Jews are more loyal to Israel than to Ireland, 36% think Jews have too much power in business, 31% opine that Jews don't care about anyone but their own kind and are hated because of the way they behave (poll conducted in December 2024 by M. Inbari and K. Bumin). Furthermore, 11.3% of Irish Christians support Israel in their fight by contrast with 43.3% of adults in the USA; 45.6% of the Irish support the Palestinians, but only 11.2% Americans.

6 Guterres (b. 1949) was prime minister of Portugal (1995–2002), a socialist and devout Catholic, president of the Socialist International 1999–2005, UN High Commissioner for Refugees 2005–15, Secretary General of UN since 2016.

7   Guterres, although fond of invoking international law when casti-
    gating Israel, seems unaware of the fact that according to international
    law, Israel is not an occupying power in the 'West Bank' (Judaea and
    Samaria). According to the principle *uti possidetus iuris*, a newly formed
    independent sovereign state inherits the undivided boundaries of the
    precedent state if no other state has a recognized claim to it. Since the
    Palestinians and the Arab League rejected the offer of a Palestinian state
    in part of Mandated Palestine, choosing to invade instead, the only state
    to replace the Mandate was Israel. According to international law, Israel
    is not an occupier in Judaea and Samaria.

8   First, in 1947, when the British withdrew from the British Mandate
    of Palestine, Ben Gurion offered peace to all Arab neighbours, but the
    Kingdom of Jordan, Kingdom of Egypt, Syria, and Lebanon all invaded,
    each seeking to grab what territory they could and to slaughter the Jews.
    Second, in 2000, Israeli Prime Minister Ehud Barak met Yasir Arafat,
    terrorist leader of the Palestine Liberation Organisation, at Camp David,
    under the chairmanship of US President Bill Clinton and offered Arafat
    94% of the West Bank with East Jerusalem (but not the Old City) as its
    capital and the Gaza Strip. Clinton later said, 'Arafat was here for 14 days
    and said No to everything'. Arafat then launched the first Intifada, in
    which over a thousand Israeli civilians were killed and thousands more
    mutilated by suicide-bombers and suitcase bombs placed on buses.
    Third, in 2008, Ehud Olmert offered Mahmoud Abbas even more than
    Barak had offered Arafat, but this too was turned down.

9   The term 'Nakba' (catastrophe) is now used by anti-Zionists and by
    Palestinian Arabs to suggest that the 'catastrophe' of the Palestinian
    refugees was the result of the creation of the State of Israel, rather than
    the result of the failure of the attack on the nascent State of Israel by
    Jordan, Iraq, Lebanon, Saudi Arabia, and Egypt whose explicit purpose
    was to overwhelm and destroy the state of Israel in 1947/8.

10 'The Protokols of the Elders of Zion' was a Russian forgery published
    in *Znamya*, a Black Hundreds (fascist) newspaper owned by Pavel
    Kushevan (initiator of the Kishinev progroms), compiled by two Russian
    journalists at the direction of Pyotr Rachovsky, chief of Russian secret
    service in Paris. It purports to be the minutes of a late nineteenth cen-
    tury meeting of Jewish leaders, plotting to control the world. It is one of
    the most successful antisemitic tracts ever written, being circulated in
    hundreds of millions of copies by Tsarist Russia, the USSR, the Nazis,
    the Muslims (especially Muhammad Amin Husseini), and post USSR
    Russia. It provided favourite reading for Czar Nicholas II and his wife
    Alexandra, who were extreme antisemites.

11 See analysis by former BBC TV Director, Danny Cohen, calling for an
    independent enquiry into the BBC's coverage of the Israel/Hamas war.

A similar critical report on the BBC biased and inaccurate reporting was published by British/Israeli lawyer Trevor Asserson. There has been no such independent enquiry.

12 In the USA there are dozens of Palestinian organizations planning and funding demonstrations and university sit-ins, financially supported by a wide range of (sometimes innocent) bodies, e.g. the Rockefeller Brothers Fund, The Open Society Foundation, Tides Foundation. Qatar contributed $13 billion to American universities and colleges between 2001 and 2021, often undeclared and concealed. Recipient institutions exhibited much increased antisemitism on their campuses ('Antizionist faculty barometer': AMCHAinitiative.org; 'On academic indoctrination in American universities': jno.org [November 2, 2024]). I shall not explore in any detail the origins of traditional Muslim antisemitism in the Quran, or the roots of modern Muslim antisemitism, which lie in Nazi propaganda, on the one hand, and extensive Soviet and Russian antisemitic propaganda that has been going on since long before the foundation of the State of Israel. That has been dealt with comprehensively by J.W. Simons, *Israelophobia: The Newest Version of the Oldest Hatred and What to do about it* (Constable, London, 2023).

13 G. Wright, S. Hecht, S. Volodarsky, L. Saxe, 'Antisemitism on Campus: Understanding Hostility to Jews and Israel', Cohen Centre for Jewish Studies, Brandeis University, August 2024.

3 Antisemitism

A Historical Sketch[1]

1. *Antisemitism: ancient hatred and intolerance* Antisemitism is the longest lasting hatred in the world. Jews have been hated because they are too rich and because they are too poor; because they are capitalists and because they are communists; because they keep to themselves and because they infiltrate everywhere in society; because they believe tenaciously in an old and transcended faith linked to their ancestral homeland of Israel and its capital Jerusalem and because they are rootless cosmopolitans who believe nothing; because they do not speak properly the language of the country in which they dwell and because they speak it too well.

Human beings are tribal, xenophobic animals. Any deficiency in our sense of identity is commonly compensated for by finding an object of hatred, either within our society or external to it. This often is exacerbated by religious and ideological belief systems which encourage bigotry, prejudice, and self-righteousness. Group violence and destruction sustained by ideology and led by a charismatic leader give meaning to otherwise empty lives. Human beings, when their evil propensities are unleashed, enjoy destruction, rape and murder, as well as a momentarily liberating loss of identity in mob behaviour. This has been manifested countless times in wars of religion and in civil wars, as well as in the recurrent slaughter of Jews.

2. *Peculiarity of Jewish faith* The Jews in the ancient world were a decidedly strange people. They worshipped one god and one god alone, rejecting all the multitudinous gods of others. Moreover, they did not erect any statues to their god, although they made sacrifices to him just like any normal mortals. But their god was invisible and unrepresentable, a thought that defied intelligibility for most pagans.

DOI: 10.4324/9781003711957-3

Moreover, his name, represented by the Hebrew letters 'Yhvh', was too sacred to be pronounced. This too must have seemed bizarre. They had peculiar dietary laws, which meant that they would not sit down to eat with other people – a practice that must have appeared offensive to say the least. They seemed to hold themselves aloof from others, to be intensely argumentative and quarrelsome, and to enjoy a higher literacy rate than other societies around them (as shown by recent archaeological evidence of ostraca from 600BC in Tel Arad). None of this was likely to endear them to their neighbours.

3. *Seleucid antisemitism* Antisemitism was evident in the ancient world. It was patent in the savage onslaught on Judaea by Antiochus IV Epiphanes ('God Manifest', ruler of the Seleucid empire from 175 to 164BC), determined to eradicate the Jewish faith and force Judaeans to worship him as a god. His conquest of Jerusalem and desecration of the Second Temple provoked the Maccabean revolt, led by the five sons of Mattathias of Modi'in (including Judas Maccabeus, who, like three of his brothers, died heroically in battle), and lasting from 167 to 134BC, when Simon, the last of the brothers, finally overthrew the Seleucid yoke. Antisemitism was no less patent in Egypt, where there were extensive Jewish communities. Particularly vicious were the writings of Manetho (third century BC) – who referred to the Jews as a 'race of lepers' expelled from Egypt, and Apion, a Hellenized Egyptian in the first half of the first century AD, whose writings included a libel of Jewish cannibalism. His rantings were sufficiently widely read for Josephus Flavius to write *Against Apion* – a polemical response to these calumnies.

4. *Roman destruction of Judaea and collective punishment of the Jews* The most important source of ancient (pre-Christian) antisemitism emerged from the Jewish revolt of 67AD and its savage repression by Vespasian and his son Titus. The revolt was precipitated by the incompetence and cruelty of the insignificant Roman governor Gessius Florus in Caesarea Maritima, who failed to protect the local Jews from some louts who had provocatively sacrificed a cockerel outside the synagogue. Subsequently, Gessius Florus, coming to Jerusalem to collect taxes and confronted by an indignant and resentful crowd, loosed his troops upon them. They massacred 3,600 men, women, and children, crucified and scourged Jews of Roman equestrian rank, contrary to Roman law. Unsurprisingly, a local revolt broke out, which rapidly developed into an irrational, because hopeless, attempt to attain independence from Rome. Cestius Gallus, governor of Roman

Syria, marched to restore order in 66AD. Inflicting heavy losses upon the Jerusalemites, he fought his way successfully through Jerusalem to the very gates of the Temple. Then, perhaps thinking he had adequately demonstrated Roman might, he decided to withdraw. This was catastrophic. His attempted withdrawal through the wadis leading to Jerusalem was a debacle in which he lost 5,300 infantry and 480 cavalry, as well as all his siege equipment. This made a major war inevitable. Nero allocated the task to Vespasian, a relatively undistinguished general, and his son Titus. They gathered a huge force of sixty thousand men in Ptolomais (Acre) in 67AD, but as a result of the suicide of Nero and the turbulent year of the four emperors (69AD),[2] the actual siege of Jerusalem was postponed, although the revolt in the countryside was savagely suppressed. Vespasian, declared emperor by his own troops, had no legitimate claim to the throne. He badly needed a major military victory and a consequent triumph in Rome to establish a new dynasty in place of the Julio-Claudian one. So it was indispensable for him to demonstrate that the revolt in Judaea was actually a threat to the Roman empire and that its suppression merited a triumph. It is this which explains the uniqueness of the Roman destruction of Jerusalem[3] and of Judaea – it is the only case in Roman history in which a century-old Roman province, the source of substantial tax income to the state, was deliberately destroyed by the Romans themselves. One immediate result, which was to have dire long-term consequences, was that Titus enforced a collective punishment on the Jews throughout the empire (irrespective of any involvement in the Judaean revolt) to pay a per capita tax of two drachma to the temple of Jupiter Capitolinus in Rome, equivalent to the annual contribution that Jews throughout the empire had voluntarily paid to the Temple in Jerusalem to support the religious ceremonies and sacrifices there. This meant that Roman tax collectors required detailed lists of all Jews in the empire, which ensured that it was public knowledge who was a Jew and was therefore incurring punishment for the revolt that was crushed by Vespasian and Titus in 70AD.[4] This itself was a potent source of subsequent antisemitic feelings. The Jews were forbidden to rebuild their temple, which was itself an unprecedented punishment. The subsequent desperate revolt of Bar Kokhva in 132–5AD that was brutally crushed by Hadrian, led to the levelling of Jerusalem and the building of the Roman city of *Aeolia Capitolina* on its site. The very name 'Judaea' was erased, and was replaced by 'Palestina', a Latinization of 'Philistia', the land of the Philistines, an Aegean sea-people who had settled on the southern Canaanite coast around 1175BC forming a confederation of small city states such as Ashdod, Ekron, Gath, Ashkelon, Azah (Gaza), and who subsequently vanished from history after being conquered in the early sixth century BC by the Emperor Nebuchadnezzar II and exiled to Babylon.

5. *Early Christian antisemitism: Jews as deicides* The next phase of antisemitism was early Christian. It did not originate from Jews who had converted to Christianity (there were numerous Jewish sects in the first century that tolerated each other), but from gentiles who had adopted Christianity. It was not rooted in the preaching of Jesus, who was no more than a traditional Jewish prophet much influenced by the great pre-rabbinic teacher Hillel the Elder, the Pharisees and possibly the Essenes, seeking not to reform, let alone to overthrow, Judaism, but to urge Jews to live up to the moral and religious standards of their forefathers. The creator of Christianity was Paul. His converts increasingly distanced themselves from Judaism, despite claiming to recognize the same God and employing the Jewish bible as their so-called 'Old Testament' that presaged and prefigured the 'New Testament'. The early Church fathers turned against Jews and Judaism with increasing vitriol, characterizing Jews as deicides and evolving a wide battery of spurious contrasts between the Old and the New Testaments. They developed an extensive battery of doctrine *Contra Judeos*. The God of the Old Testament was a god of wrath and vengeance, the God (the same god) of the New Testament was the god of mercy. Judaism was a hide-bound religion of law, Christianity was a religion of love (although it accepted the Mosaic Ten Commandments). Jews were vengeful, in as much as they cleaved to the *lex talionis* instead of being merciful (whereas both the Pentateuch and the rabbinical interpretations reject any literal interpretation of the Babylonian (Hammurabian) *lex talionis*). Jews hold themselves to be the Chosen People, while according to the early Church fathers, they are an accursed people. In fact, Jews held themselves to be chosen to be 'a holy people', subject to stricter and more extensive laws than the *jus gentium* that applied to gentiles. This form of antisemitism reached its zenith in the fourth century writings of St Jerome and St John Chrysostom ('golden tongued'), both still venerated and studied in Catholic and Greek Orthodox Christianity. The 'golden tongue' of St John was exhibited above all in his vituperative diatribes against the 'evil Jewish deicides'.

6. *Demonization of Jews by crusaders – origins of blood-libel* The third transmutation of antisemitism is the demonization of Jews and of Judaism at the time of the Crusades. The First Crusade of 1096 was accompanied by extensive slaughter of Jews, especially in the Rhineland, at Speyer, Worms, and Mainz, as well as Cologne, Mehr, and Geldern under the leadership of Count Emich of Flonheim.[5] The immediate motivation was plunder, rape and the joy of slaughter, but the ideological motivation was vengeance upon the Jews for deicide. The Jews had killed Jesus, was the doctrine, and therefore, since the crusaders were on their way to the Holyland to capture it from the Muslims whom they intended to kill, it was incumbent upon them to kill as many Jews on the way as possible too.[6] This phase of antisemitism involved not theological disputation against Judaism, but the demonization of Jews. The bloodlibel originated in England in the alleged ritual murder by Jews (that supposedly re-enacted the scourging and crucifixion of Christ) of a Saxon boy named William in Norwich in 1144. This was a tale concocted by a Benedictine monk Thomas of Monmouth in 1150 in order to create a local shrine, dedicated to 'little St William' whose shrine would work miracles for pilgrims donating gifts to the church. This led to a flurry of similar tales throughout England (Harold of Gloucester 1168; Robert of Bury 1181; Hugh of Lincoln 1255) that were embedded in English literature by Geoffrey Chaucer in the singularly repulsive 'The Prioress's Tale' in his *Canterbury Tales* c. 1400 (written long after the expulsion of Jews from England by Edward I in 1296). This made a major contribution to English demonization of Jews in literature, from Marlowe and Shakespeare to Dickens's Fagin.[7] The blood libel received further embroidery in Fulda, Germany in 1235 where it was alleged that Jews needed the blood of Christian children to make mazzah (unleavened bread) at Passover. This libel had widespread and long-lasting appeal and still flourishes in Arab countries. It was closely linked to the Catholic literal understanding of the taking of the sacrament (the transubstantiation of consecrated wine and wafer into the blood and body of Christ) and to the Catholic obsession with the desecration of the host. Members of a Catholic congregation who took the sacrament could give quietus to their qualms about cannibalism (literal or symbolic) by reflecting on the fact that the hated Jews actually drank the blood of Christians.[8] This was bizarre indeed, since the laws of the Jewish faith, unlike the rules of Christian faith, forbid the consumption of blood in any form.

7. *Luther's ferocious antisemitism* The demonization of Jews was exacerbated by the outbreak of the Black Death in the mid-fourteenth century, when the Jews, sometimes less infected by plague than Christians, given their frequent bathing and washing of hands before each meal, were accused of poisoning the wells from which Christians drank. This form of demonization of Jews lasted for centuries. It informed Luther's ferocious antisemitism in the sixteenth century. In his book *Von den Juden und ihren Lüger* (1543), Luther demanded that all Jewish synagogues and schools should be burnt down; all prayer books be destroyed; rabbis forbidden to teach; Jewish houses be burnt down; all property and money confiscated; all legal protection be abolished; Jews be drafted into forced labour or be expelled forever. This culminated in the declaration 'We are at fault for not slaying them'. Small wonder that in Nazi Germany, four hundred years later, Goebbels remarked that all the Nazis were doing to the Jews was what Luther had suggested should be done.

8. *Enlightenment antisemitism* The fourth transmutation of antisemitism occurs with the eighteenth and nineteenth century Enlightenment. A movement dedicated to the cultivation of reason, liberation from the Catholic Church, adoption of deism if not atheism, and rejection of bigotry and dogma, might be expected to be free of antisemitism. But it evidently takes more than a slogan: 'sapere aude'[9] to shed two thousand years of bigotry. Voltaire was an antisemite, writing in his *Dictionnaire Philosophique*, 'we find in them only an ignorant and barbarous people, who have long united the most sordid avarice with the most detestable superstition and the most invincible hatred for every people by whom they are tolerated and enriched.' Kant himself, despite his friendship with the distinguished Jewish philosopher Moses Mendelsohn, rarely missed an opportunity to characterize Jews as 'vile', 'cowardly', 'liars', 'cheats', 'vampires of society' and to denigrate the Jewish Bible. Lessing, especially in his play 'Nathan the Wise', was a happy exception to the rule. Late eighteenth century and early nineteenth century German philosophers went from bad to worse. Fichte objected vehemently to granting civil rights to Jews, asserting that the only solution to the Jewish problem was to 'cut off their heads'. Hegel held that Judaism was the prototype of a slave morality. Schopenhauer claimed that Jews were 'no better than cattle'.

9. *Ethnic antisemitism* The fifth transmutation, primarily in nineteenth century Germany and Austria, from where it spread over most of

Western Europe, initiated ethnic antisemitism as opposed to religious antisemitism in its various forms. Jews were to be hated not because of their faith and their failure to accept the tenets of Catholic Christianity or of Lutheran Protestantism, but because they were a separate and degenerate race. This doctrine implied that the alleged evil traits of the Jews were genetic. Consequently, conversion to Christianity was irrelevant in as much as no Jew could possibly be a Christian, for the evil traits of the Jews were hereditary. Intermarriage was therefore to be prohibited, for a Jewish spouse would contaminate pure Aryan (French, German, Anglo-Saxon, etc.) blood.

This dark doctrine had been anticipated in Spain in the fifteenth-century doctrine of 'the cleanliness of blood' or 'blood purity' (*limpieza de sangre*). It was prominent in the persecution of the Marranos (converted Jews) who were suspected of continuing to practice their original faith in secret, and it became pivotal to the activities of the Spanish Inquisition after the expulsion of the Jews in 1492. It persisted in Spain, in one form or another, well into the nineteenth century.[10]

10. *19th century antisemitism* Ethnic antisemitism resurfaced in nine-teenth century Austria and Germany, being advanced by Georg von Schönerer (1842–1921) and then Karl Lueger, mayor of Vienna from 1892 until 1910, whose antisemitism appears to have been largely opportunistic. Leading racial antisemites in Germany were Richard Wagner; the Prussian economist Eugen Duehring (1833–1921), who advocated the 'murder and extermination' of the Jews; Paul de Lagarde (1827–91), a German biblical scholar who was a precursor of the Nazis; and the Anglo-German Houston Stewart Chamberlain (1855–1927), a staunch Wagnerian and much taken with the antisemitism of the composer. France, to be sure, was not to be left behind. The French Revolution granted the emancipation of the Jews and Napoleon had enforced it throughout the Germanic lands he conquered. With his fall, the reinstated *ancien regime* reversed his legislation. The leading French antisemitic figure in the latter half of the nineteenth century was Éduard Drumont (1844–1917), who initiated the *Ligue natio-nale anti-sémitique de France* and was founder and editor of the antisemitic newspaper *La Libre Parole* which was the major anti-Dreyfusard catalyst.

Racial, ethnic, antisemitism received a boost from the late nineteenth-century perversion of Darwinian evolutionary theory, namely social Darwinism. Its advocates viewed history as a competition for survival among races, in which only the fittest would survive. The alleged inferiority of the Jewish race meant that they were destined to be exterminated for the benefit of mankind as a whole, whose blood was purer and whose intellect was superior.[11]

11. *Rise of Nazism* Racial antisemitism laid the scene for the Nazi Holocaust, in which six million Jews were systematically slaughtered, while the rest of the world stood by indifferently, or worse, when countries occupied by the Third Reich actively cooperated with the Nazi 'Final Solution'. In the late 1930s, as the Nazi savagery towards Jews was becoming evident, the rest of the world watched, unwilling to provide safe haven for the Jews.

One redeeming feature in Britain was the foundation of the Academic Assistance Council in 1933 under the chairmanship of the Director of the London School of Economics, William Beveridge. Its aim was to find academic and other institutions to provide places for professors, teachers, doctors, judges, lawyers, civil servants, and musicians dismissed from their posts by Nazi legislation. It was renamed The Society for the Protection of Science and Learning in 1936. By 1939 they had aided at least 900 people to escape from the clutches of the Nazis and to find posts in the UK or Australia and New Zealand. Many went on to become the Nobel Prize winners. The main opposition to their efforts came from the British medical and dental associations, from Whitehall and the Home Office.

12. *British Mandate record* Nevertheless, Britain's record was lamentable. Many Jews would have fled to the British Mandate in Palestine, set up by the League of Nations as a national home for the Jews in 1922. But, as the threat of war loomed, the British Prime Minister, the arch-appeaser Neville Chamberlain, eager to curry favour with the Arabs in the Middle East, issued a White Paper in April,1939, violating all the commitments Britain had made to the League of Nations (which had set up the British Mandate) and strictly limiting Jewish immigration precisely when a refuge was most needed. Winston Churchill addressed the House of Commons on the issue on May 22, 1939, saying that as one intimately and responsibly concerned in the earlier stages of our Palestine policy[12], he could not 'stand by and see solemn engagements into which Britain has entered before the world set aside. . . .What will our potential enemies think? Will they not be tempted to say "They're on the run again. This is another Munich."' Addressing Chamberlain directly, Churchill reminded the Prime Minister that twenty years earlier, in the House of Commons,

Chamberlain had said, 'A great responsibility will rest upon the Zionists, who, before long will be proceeding with joy in their hearts, to the ancient seat of their people. Theirs will be the task to build up a new prosperity and a new civilization in an old Palestine, so long neglected and misruled.' 'Well,' Churchill continued, 'they have answered his call. They have fulfilled his hopes. How can he find it in his heart to strike them this mortal blow?'[13] In July 1939, the British colonial secretary Malcolm MacDonald announced that all Jewish immigration to Palestine would be suspended from October 1939 until March 1940. After Kristallnacht in November 1938, the UK allowed ten thousand Jewish children to find refuge in Britain *but would not allow their parents to accompany them*. Nor was the British government willing to provide any financial support for the operation – on the contrary, the Home Office demanded a downpayment of £50 for each child (equivalent to £4,300 in 2025) to cover education and repatriation after three years as well as demanding a guaranteed home for each child. The funds were raised by Jewish organizations and the Quakers. By the outbreak of war, Britain had admitted a mere 70,000, mainly Jewish, refugees from the Nazis on condition they had guaranteed jobs as servants (so as not to jeopardize British employment). On the continent, the Jews who could not escape were doomed. After France was overrun in 1940, when the Nazis demanded that Vichy France send Jewish adults to the death camps in Poland, the French government under Laval and Petain asked the Germans to take the children as well.

13. *Nazi holocaust: definition of genocide* The Nazi Holocaust during the Second World War consisted in the genocidal slaughter of six million Jews, including one and a half million children. The term 'genocide' was coined by the Jewish jurist Rafael Lemkin in 1943 with regard to the Ittihadist (Young Turks) mass slaughter of the Armenians in Turkey by Tala'at Bey and Enver Pasha during the First World War. It was adopted as a legal term in international law by the United Nations in 1948, as was the term 'crimes against humanity' introduced by Professor Hersch Lauterpacht, Jewish professor of international law at Cambridge University. 'Genocide' in international law is a crime with intent – genocide being defined as acts committed with the intent to destroy, in whole or in part, a national, ethnic, racial, or religious group by (a) killing members of the group; (b) causing serious bodily or mental harm to members of the group; (c) deliberately inflicting on the group conditions of life calculated to bring about

its physical destruction in whole or in part; (d) imposing measures intended to prevent births within the group; (e) forcibly transferring children of the group to another group.

Other instances of genocide in the twentieth century are the German slaughter of the Herero and Nama tribes in German South-West Africa (1904–8) in which approximately 110,000 were murdered; the slaughter of some 150,000 Jews by Denikin's White Russian Cossacks during the Russian civil war in the early 1920s; the USSR Holodomor in Ukraine in the 1930s when seven million Ukrainian kulaks were killed by deliberate starvation; the Nigerian-Biafran civil war of 1967–70 in which between one and three million Biafrans were killed; the East Timor slaughter by Indonesia between 1975 and 1999 (approximately 200,000 dead); the massacre of the Tamils by the Sinhalese in Sri Lanka (Ceylon) between 1983 and 2009 (approximately 80,000–100,000 civilian deaths, extensive rape of women and abduction of children); the slaughter of the Tutsi in Rwanda in 1994 in which more than half a million Tutsi were murdered and between a quarter and half a million women were raped; the current forcible detainment of approximately a million Moslem Uyghars in internment camps in Xianjing by chairman Xi Jinping, accompanied by forced labour, compulsory sterilization, and persecution; the forced settlement of Chinese in Tibet and the deliberate destruction of traditional Tibetan Buddhist culture, again under the directives of Xi Jinping.

14. *Uniqueness of Nazi holocaust* Given the multiplicity of genocides in the twentieth century, it is common, as has already been noted, for anti-Zionists to remonstrate that the Jews make too much fuss of the Nazi Holocaust: there are lots of holocausts so there is nothing special about this Jewish one! As we shall see, this sentiment plays an important role in some variants of anti-Zionism. So it is important to make it clear that the Nazi genocide of the Jews of Europe, Western Russia, and Ukraine was, indeed, unique. This is not merely because of its scale and extreme cruelty. Eight features are conjunctively decisive. (i) The systematic bureaucratic organization of the Holocaust with meticulous records kept. (ii) The transportation of millions of victims over huge distances for the sole purpose of murdering them (e.g. from the Pyrenees to Auschwitz). (iii) The diversion of transport, funding, and manpower from the war effort in 1943–5 for the purpose of slaughtering the Jews of Europe. (iv) The technology and mechanization of slaughter in the death camps. (v) The industrialization and commercialization of death, e.g. hair shorn from women

for upholstery before gassing, gold teeth extracted from corpses for bullion, bones used for manufacture of soap. (vi) Its universality, namely the slaughter of all Jews in all captured territories. (vii) The fact that it occurred in one of the most civilized nations of Europe, the lands of Bach, Mozart, and Beethoven, of Goethe and Schiller, of Dürer and Cranach. (viii) That it explicitly aimed at the destruction of the moral order of humanity.

15. *Judaism: a religion of hope and of celebration of life* It would be altogether mistaken to suppose that this long and terrible history of persecution has led the Jewish people to have a permanent sense of victimhood. Nothing could be further from the truth. Judaism is a religion of a people who conceive of themselves as being constantly tested by God, knowing that they are free to choose to obey the moral law or to disobey, knowing that the future is open and not preordained. That is why tragedy characterizes the ancient Greek view of human life but is alien to the ancient Hebrew vision. Pelagius (354–418AD), a clear thinking and clear-headed British theologian, was much closer to Jewish theology than Augustine of Hippo (354–430), who believed in original sin and predestination. Pelagius denied both and was anathematized for his beliefs. The Jewish faith is full of hope for the future. It is not for nothing that the very first Jewish settlement established in 1878 was called 'Petach Tikvah', the Gateway of Hope. Nor is it a coincidence that the national anthem of the State of Israel (adopted from a song written by Naftali Herz Imber in 1877) is entitled 'Hatikvah', the Hope. Judaism is also a religion of life, by contrast with the ideologies of Hamas and Iranian Shia death-cults.[14] For it is written in *Deuteronomy* 30:19, 'I have set before you life, not death, blessing and cursing: therefore choose life, that both thou and thy seed may live.' It is a religion that celebrates life.

Notes

1 In the following remarks I am indebted to the luminous writings of the late chief Rabbi of the Commonwealth, Lord Jonathan Sacks in his book *Future Tense* (Hodder and Stoughton, 2009). The account I offer differs from his in some respects.

2 Otho, Vitellius, Galba, and Vespasian.

3 It is noteworthy that Pliny the Elder had characterized Herodian Jerusalem as the greatest city in the east, second only to Rome in its grandeur.

4 See Martin Goodman, *Rome and Jerusalem* (Penguin Books, London, 2008), Epilogue: the Origins of Antisemitism, pp. 578–585

5 See Christopher Tyerman, *A New History of the Crusades* (Penguin, London, 2007), pp. 100–106.

6 The crusader zeal in their murderous antisemitism of the first crusade presaged their later zeal in slaughtering Christians, first in their sacking of Constantinople on the fourth crusade (1204) and later in the Albigensian crusade (1209–1229) in which the barons of northern France sacked and destroyed the Languedoc (Occitane), the richest province in France. To repeat Rabbi Jonathan Sacks's profound observation, what begins with antisemitism rarely ends with antisemitism.

7 When this was pointed out to Dickens by Mrs Eliza Davis, a Jewish reader, he doctored his own text extensively. But the fact that he was barely aware of the antisemitic nature of his depiction of Fagin, is itself disturbing. In David Lean's film of *Oliver Twist*, Alec Guinness's make-up for Fagin could have come straight out of *Der Sturmer*. William Fishman, professor of local history at Queen Mary's College, London, observed that but for Fagin all the pickpocketing children would have died on the streets of London from cold and starvation.

8 The blood-libel never really died. Its most infamous resurrection in modern times was the Beiliss Affair between 1911 and 1913. Menahem Beilis, a mild and modest middle-class superintendent at a brick factory in Kiev was falsely accused of the ritual murder of a 13-year-old boy Andriy Yushchinsky, an accusation warmly supported by Tsar Nicholas II. This two-year imprisonment and subsequent trial aroused worldwide indignation at Russian antisemitism.

9 'Dare to think for yourself' – Kant's enlightenment motto.

10 Until the 1860s/70s, blood purity had to be proved for entry into the Spanish army and navy.

11 Although the Jews constitute less than 0.2% of the world population, Jews and people with at least one Jewish parent have been awarded 22% of Nobel Prizes since the inception of the institution in 1901.

12 Churchill had been Secretary of State for the Colonies in the Paris Peace Conference in 1919 which established the British Mandate in Palestine decreed by the League of Nations.

13 Martin Gilbert, *Israel: A History* (Black Swan, rev. ed., London, 2008), p. 98.

14 See Douglas Murray, *On Democracies and Death Cults: Israel and the Future of Civilization* (Broadside Books, 2025).

4 The Aftermath of the Nazi Holocaust

1. *Allied inaction during the Second World War on Nazi death-camps* Although the slaughter of the Jews by the Nazis was known to the leaders of the Allies and the commanders of the Allied armed forces fighting Germany, nothing was done to stop or impede it. There was no widespread announcement that any German or Austrian official or member of the Wehrmacht or any pro-Nazi member of police forces in occupied Europe would be brought to trial and punished after the conquest of Germany. There was no attempt to bomb the railroads leading to the death-camps, although that could have been done. There was no attempt to bomb the gas chambers. The discovery of the death-camps in 1945 was indeed met with utter horror. For ten to fifteen years thereafter, antisemitism was, for the most part, silenced in the West (although not in Muslim lands of the Middle-East, where the Grand Mufti of Jerusalem Muhammad Amin Husseini continued to spread Nazi genocidal doctrine). Genocide and crimes against humanity were enshrined in international legal conventions in 1948 in the hope that no Jewish or any other holocaust could ever happen again.

2. *Amin Husseini, Grand Mufti of Jerusalem, promises Hitler to slaughter all Jews in Palestine* Mohammad Amin Husseini, who had been appointed Grand Mufti of Jerusalem by the British in 1921, fled from the British to avoid arrest for his part in the anti-British Arab rebellion in 1936. He visited Germany in 1941 and promised Hitler that when Rommel conquered the Palestine Mandate, his followers in the country would exterminate every single Jew. He wrote,

> Our fundamental condition for cooperating with Germany was a free hand to eradicate the very last Jew from Palestine and the

DOI: 10.4324/9781003711957-4

Arab world. I asked Hitler for an explicit undertaking to allow us to solve the Jewish problem in a manner befitting our national and racial aspirations and according to the scientific methods innovated by Germany in its handling of its Jews. The answer I got was 'The Jews are yours'.

He ensured widespread circulation of an Arabic translation of *Mein Kampf* in the Middle East and North Africa. To this day, the book is widely sold all across the Middle East. A well-read and underlined copy of the book was found in a children's room used as a base by Hamas terrorists in the Gaza strip in 2023. It was displayed to the BBC interviewer Laura Kuenssberg by President Herzog (the President of Israel) in a video interview on November 12, 2023.

3. *Anti-Zionism and antisemitism of Attlee government 1945–1950*
The anti-Zionism and antisemitism of the Attlee government after the war continued unabated, quite explicitly in the case of the foreign secretary Ernest Bevin and the Colonial Secretary Creech Jones. The last British High Commissioner for Palestine, Sir Alan Cunningham described Zionism as a movement in which 'the forces of nationalism are accompanied by the psychology of the Jew, which it is important to recognize as something quite abnormal and unresponsive to rational treatment.'[1] British unwillingness to admit Jewish survivors into the Palestine Mandate was overridden by the UNSCOP[2] recommendations in 1947 that proposed an end to the Mandate, the immediate admission of 100,000 Jewish Holocaust survivors into Palestine, and the division of Palestine into two small states, one Jewish and the other Arab, with Jerusalem internationalized under the UN (see Map 4). The Palestinian Jews immediately accepted the proposal, the Palestinian Arabs and the Arab High Committee, the Arab League, and Arab States (Trans-Jordan, Iraq, Syria, Lebanon, Egypt, Saudi Arabia) all rejected it. Five Arab armies invaded, none with the aim of setting up a state for Palestinian Arabs. Their aim was simply to prevent the establishment of a Jewish state and to grab territory for themselves. The Israel War of Independence ensued, resulting, against all odds, in the triumph of the nascent State of Israel. Holocaust survivors, having been kept (by the Allies) in displaced persons camps in Europe for longer than any other survivors from Nazi terror, and in internment camps in Cyprus (by the British), were at last able to find a home.

4. *Holocaust-guilt weariness among gentiles* With time, however, the world got tired of the Holocaust. Already in 2002, Portuguese Nobel

Laureate José Saramago wrote 'the Jews endlessly scratch their own wound to keep it bleeding, to make it incurable, and they show it to the world as if it were a banner. ... Israel wants all of us to feel guilty, directly or indirectly, for the horrors of the Holocaust.' Significant numbers of the public in Western societies find that Jews make too much of the Holocaust (after all, there are so many holocausts!) or contend that Jews try to use the Holocaust to Jewish advantage. One third of British Christians currently believe that Jews 'talk too much' about the Holocaust and 47% of them believe that Israel committed genocide in Gaza (February 2025).[3] One third of the Irish think Jews talk too much about the Holocaust (similar poll, December 2024). One might indeed say that many people cannot forgive Jews for the Holocaust! Holocaust guilt has become wearisome. Claiming that Israel is committing genocide in the Gaza strip, that it is doing to the Gazans what the Nazis did to the Jews, relieves some gentiles of any feelings of guilt, since the Israelis, and by implication Jews in general, are just as bad as the Nazis. This was patent in the demonstrations and graffiti throughout the West in 2024/5, in which the Israeli flag was commonly held up with a swastika placed in the middle of the Star of David.

5. *Jeremy Corbyn, leader of Labour Party UK, legitimizes overt anti-semitism* Antisemitism, in the thin guise of anti-Zionism, became legitimate in some circles in Britain through Jeremy Corbyn, leader of the British Labour party 2015–2020. Under his leadership, the Labour Party was characterized by institutionalized racism and anti-semitism and condemned as such. The British Equality and Human Rights Commission presented a report in which it asserted that there had been 'unlawful acts of harassment and discrimination [against Jews] for which the Labour party is responsible' (p.6 of its report). The only other party that has been similarly condemned is the British National Party (BNP – a neo-Nazi fascist party). Remarkably, Margaret Hodge, a distinguished Jewish Labour MP, said that she had faced more antisemitism from Labour than from the BNP in her con-stituency in Barking. In August 2018, Corbyn went to Tunisia to lay a wreath on the monument honouring the perpetrators of the 1972 mas-sacre of the Israeli athletes at the Munich Olympics. He supported and donated money to terrorists, holocaust deniers, and antisemitic con-spiracy theorists. His closest colleagues, John McDonnell (Shadow Chancellor) and his parliamentary private secretary Naseem Shah (Shadow Minister of Justice) were antisemitic, as was his erstwhile colleague in parliament Ken Livingstone (MP 1987–2001), later

mayor of London (2000–2008). To be sure, they all denied they were antisemites, insisting that they were just pro-Palestinian anti-Zionists. Regarding one of Corbyn's remarks about British Jews, the chief Rabbi of the Commonwealth Lord Jonathan Sacks, said in an interview with the *New Statesman* that it was

> the most offensive statement made by a senior British politician since Enoch Powell's 1968 "rivers of blood" speech. It was divisive, hateful and, like Powell's speech, it undermines the existence of an entire group of British citizens by depicting them as essentially alien. We can only judge Jeremy Corbyn by his words and his actions. He has given support to racists, terrorists, and dealers of hate who want to kill Jews and remove Israel from the map.

Corbyn had also welcomed terrorists from the Provisional IRA into the Commons two weeks after the Brighton bombing that had aimed to kill Margaret Thatcher and her cabinet. According to John Gray, writing in 2017, Corbynite socialism appealed not so much to the traditional working class, but to 'the material and psychological needs of the relatively affluent and well-heeled', as well as to university students, who are mostly middle class. He won more votes in the general elections of 2017 and 2019 than the Labour Party in 2024. Corbyn's neo-Marxist antisemitism was distinctly bourgeois. Corbyn's successor as leader of the Party, the current Prime Minister Keir Starmer, went to great lengths to rid the Labour Party of such neo-Marxist, anti-colonialist, antisemites.

6. *Sadiq Khan's thoughtless anti-Zionism/antisemitism* However, Corbyn and his comrades are not alone in their mindless anti-Zionism. The current, much honoured, mayor of London, Sadiq Khan, in his Eid message to London Muslims at the end of Ramadan on March 30, 2025, as a casual aside, expressed his sorrow at the death of 50,000 Palestinians who had been killed by Israelis in a 'betrayal of humanity'. He made no mention of the fact that these are Hamas's totally unreliable figures, or that these figures are figures of total deaths in Gaza, including deaths by natural causes (statistically, for a population of more than two million, approximately 11,000 a year), and that it includes terrorists (approximately 20,000) killed by the IDF. These figures alone reduce his figure of 50,000 deaths to 19,000. Sadiq Khan failed to point out that his figure also includes those Gazans killed by

terrorist rockets falling short as well as civilians shot by Hamas in order to encourage them not to move to safe areas. Moreover, Sadiq Khan did not even mention the fact that the Gaza War was initiated by a savage genocidal onslaught on Israel and Israeli civilians. Nor did he mention Hamas's taking of hostages, including women, children and babies, as well as old age pensioners. All he did was to add fuel to the hatred of Israel and of Jews, who, he asserted 'betray humanity'.[4]

Notes

1 'Palestine: Future Policy', Secret Memorandum by the Secretary of State for the Colonies, Jan. 16, 1947, Annex I, CAB 129/16, C.P. (47)31).

2 'United Nations Special Committee on Palestine' set up on May 15, 1947, at the request of the UK.

3 Poll published in February 2025, with a sample of two thousand, conducted by Professor Inbari from the University of North Carolina and K. Bumin of Boston University.

4 For a reply to Sadiq Khan, see Jonathan Sacerdoti, 'Sadiq Khan's Eid message is a disgrace', *The Spectator*, April 2, 2025.

5   The Gaza Strip

1. *The Gaza Strip before 1948* Very few of those who remonstrate and demonstrate about Israel's war against Hamas, who are the elected rulers of the Gaza Strip, have any idea why the Gaza Strip exists at all. The Secretary General of the UN, Antonio Guterres is happy to announce, as we have seen, that 'the Palestinian people have been subjected to 56 years of suffocating occupation', without adverting to the question of why there is an Arab population in the Gaza Strip in the first place, as well as wrongly suggesting that Israel is occupying the Gaza Strip, when it withdrew from Gaza during the premiership of Ariel Sharon in 2005. So some historical facts need to be clarified.

What is now called the 'Gaza Strip' was, in the days of the Ottoman empire, known as Gazze, and was part of the Sanjak of Jerusalem (see Map 5). In the last Ottoman census of 1914, its population was 77,296. After the First World War, Gaza became part of the British Mandate of Palestine set up by the League of Nations. It was governed by the British until 1948 as an integral part of the Mandated territory. The British withdrew from the Palestine Mandate in 1948, leaving chaos behind and giving every advantage they could to the Arab, as opposed to the Jewish, Palestinians (e.g. handing over as many of the Tegart or Taggart forts[1] as they could to the Arabs).

2. *Gaza Strip under Egyptian rule 1948–1967* King Farouk of Egypt joined Jordan, Syria and Lebanon in the scramble for ex-Mandated territory and invaded the land of Israel from the south. The IDF threw back the Egyptian forces from the Negev but was unable to evict them from their occupation of Gaza. The population of Gaza was swollen to 200,000, more than half of whom were Palestinian who had fled from

DOI: 10.4324/9781003711957-5

the fighting around Ramle and Latrun, doing their best, as any civilians would, to keep out of the path of the warring parties in the south-eastern part of the ex-Mandated territory.[2] These Arab Palestinians should, according to international law, have been offered refuge in Egypt, but the Egyptians kept them locked up in the Gaza strip, issuing them with All-Palestine passports (paying lip-service to the existence of an All-Palestinian Government that had been proclaimed in 1948 by the Arab League (Egypt, Syria, Lebanon, Iraq, Saudi Arabia, Yemen[3])). It is of some interest that in December 1956, after Israel had taken the Gaza Strip from Egypt in the Sinai Campaign and before it withdrew under pressure from the USA, Golda Meir, then foreign minister of Israel, visited the Gaza Strip to see for herself the results of the Egyptian occupation. She wrote as follows:

> Then I toured the Gaza Strip from which the fedayeen[4] had gone out on their murderous assignments for so many months and in which the Egyptians had kept a quarter of a million men, women, and children (of whom nearly 60% were Arab refugees) in the most shameful poverty and destitution.
>
> I was appalled at what I saw there and by the fact that those miserable people had been maintained there in such degrading condition for over eight years only so that Arab leaders could show the refugee camps to visitors and make political capital out of them.
>
> Those refugees could and should have been resettled at once in any of the Arab countries of the Middle East – countries, incidentally, whose language and traditions and religion they share. The Arabs would still have been able to continue their quarrel with us, but at least the refugees would not have been kept in a state of semi-starvation or lived in such abject terror of their Egyptian masters.
>
> I couldn't help comparing what I saw in the Gaza Strip to what we have done – even with all the mistakes we made – for the Jews who had come to Israel in those same years.[5]

The All-Palestine government later moved from Gaza to Cairo. This fictional government was finally dissolved by Nasser in 1959. Egypt ruled the Gaza Strip as an occupying power until 1967.

3. *Gaza Strip 1967–2023* In 1967, in the Six-Day War provoked by Nasser, Israel retook the Gaza Strip as well as conquering the whole of the Sinai Peninsula. Retaking the Gaza Strip in 1967 could hardly

be characterized as a conquest in as much as it was merely evicting the Egyptians from their occupancy of a part of the Mandated territory which they had seized illegally in 1948. In fact, in 1948, the only legitimate governance of the Gaza Strip was the State of Israel. To be sure, the Gaza Strip was never a part of a Palestinian Arab state and Farouk did not invade the State of Israel in order to establish one. The Palestinian leaders had, after all, refused the offer of a state within the boundaries of the Mandate in 1948 in the hope that the Arab League would triumph in the war against the nascent Jewish state. Israel governed the Gaza Strip from 1967 until 1994, allowing Jewish settlers to establish seventeen settlements in the Strip with a Jewish population of some 8,800. In 1979, when Egypt, led by Sadat, and Israel, led by Begin, signed a peace treaty, the international border between Egypt and Israel was agreed to be the Philadelphi Corridor, but the status of Gaza remained undetermined. In the 1994 Oslo Accords, the Palestinian Authority was granted the administration of Gaza, save for the Jewish settlements. In 2005, Israeli prime minister Ariel Sharon ordered the dismantling of the Jewish settlements, removing all Jewish settlers from the Strip and handing over the administration to the Palestinian Authority, in the hope that Gaza would be turned into a thriving independent city-state on the Mediterranean coast. This, however, was not to be. Under pressure from the State Department and President George W. Bush, against the advice of Israel and the Mossad, the Palestinian Authority was made to hold an election in the Gaza Strip in 2006. As we have already described above, the Hamas alliance Reform and Change won only 42% of the votes but an overwhelming 56% of the seats. Within weeks, Hamas had murdered the majority of the officials of the Palestinian Authority in Gaza and seized control of the Strip. Instead of turning Gaza into a prosperous city-state, it bent most of its efforts to building underground tunnels with concrete reinforcements and missile launching pads by the thousands. It had nineteen years to build a unique underground city adapted to insurgency warfare. As soon as it had seized power, it proceeded regularly to fire rockets indiscriminately on Jewish towns and villages. Their inhabitants, mostly young idealist families, eager to befriend Gazans, were forced to live a life of unparalleled peril from rockets, constantly having to take refuge in shelters. The IDF fought brief campaigns against Hamas in Gaza in 2009 (Operation Cast Lead);

2012 (Operation Pillar of Defence); 2014 (Operation Protective Edge); 2021 (Operation Guardian of the Walls); each time being stopped by international pressure from destroying Hamas.

Notes

1 The Tegart forts, named after their designer Sir Charles Tegart, were built by the British in Palestine in 1938 in response to the Arab uprising, led by Muhammad Husseini, the Grand Mufti of Jerusalem. Tegart based his design on his experience of the Indian insurgency. They were built of reinforced concrete, with high walls and a watch tower and were meant to be able to withstand a siege for a month. More than seventy were built throughout the Mandated territories. They are better known as Taggart forts.

2 It follows that a significant number of current Gazans are not refugees at all, since they are descendants of the original Mandatory Arab population of Gaza itself. This included some 15,000 to 30,000 descendants of Egyptian fellahin who had fled into Gaza to escape from Muhammed Ali Pasha's conscription in Egypt between 1829 and 1848. (Muhammed Ali was the de facto ruler of Egypt from 1805 to 1848.) Nevertheless, all are classified as refugees by UNWRA and the UN.

3 But not Jordan, since King Abdullah did not want any competing claims to the 'West Bank'.

4 The fedayeen were murder squads, trained in Nasser's Egypt and sent from the Sinai border across Israel, killing civilians as they went, into Jordan, where they holed up until they returned to Egypt on another killing spree.

5 Quoted in Martin Gilbert, *Israel – A History* (Black Swan ed., Transworld Publishers, 1998), pp. 329–30. Golda Meir had been an outstanding minister for Housing at the time when Israel's population, after the War of Independence, doubled in two or three years due to the incoming Holocaust survivors and Sephardi Jews evicted from, or fleeing persecution in, North Africa and the Middle East.

6 Accusations

Genocide, Apartheid, Neo-colonialism, Racialism, and Violations of International Law

1. *Anti-Israel accusations in press, universities, and NGOs* Israel currently faces uncountably many accusations of genocide, apartheid, neo-colonialism, and racism in the Western press, TV and radio, on college campuses, and in well-funded and organized mass demonstrations around the Western and antipodean world. These accusations are multiplied and given credence by the widely respected voices of numerous national and international NGOs, such as Amnesty International, Oxfam, Save the Children Fund, Medécin sans Frontière, and the Danish Refugee Council, all of whom rushed to condemn Israel for committing crimes against humanity, or for committing genocide, or for violating international law.

2. *Accusations from NGOs*

Accusations from Amnesty International Agnès Callamard, Secretary General of Amnesty International and employee of the Office of the UN High Commissioner for Human Rights announced that 'Israel is committing genocide in the Gaza War' but failed to substantiate her case in any way.[1]

Accusations from Oxfam Oxfam's Middle East Director, Sally Abi Khalil declared, 'It is a crime against humanity for a country to unleash starvation upon a population ... Over two million people are currently surviving without access to clean water ... Israel's military has caused devastating damage to more than 80% of water.' Nevertheless, the food aid that entered Gaza amounted to more than 3,000 calories per day per head. That it was not properly distributed was wholly due to Hamas. If the steel pipes from the EU for clean water and sewerage systems in Gaza were

DOI: 10.4324/9781003711957-6

used to make rockets instead, that was a Hamas decision. If anyone was committing crimes against humanity, it was Hamas, not Israel.

Accusations from Save the Children Jason Lee, director of Save the Children Fund in Occupied Palestinian Territory (although Gaza ceased to be occupied Palestinian territory in 2005), announced as early as December 21, 2023, less than three months after Hamas began the war on Israel, that 'Deliberately denying children access to life-saving food and other essentials by restricting humanitarian aid, services and goods and pushing a population into smaller and smaller areas that lack the basics to sustain life violates international humanitarian law and could amount to a war crime. The international community must prevent "atrocity crimes" from unfolding as a moral imperative and as their legal obligation.' Jason Lee seems to know nothing about international law. There is no obligation under international law to provide food for one's enemy in the midst of a war. According to Article 23 of the 4th Geneva Convention, a warring party has an obligation to *facilitate* the supply of food and humanitarian aid *on condition that the facilitator can see no serious reason for suspecting the diversion of such aid by enemy military forces*. That is precisely what Hamas did and was seen to be doing. Nevertheless, Israel acted over and above the call of duty under international law. It allowed abundant food aid into Gaza, which it was not obligated to do. Furthermore, contrary to the allegations of Jason Lee, Israel did not push Gazans into smaller and smaller areas, but rather forewarned them which areas it was going to bomb and told them in which areas they would be safe.

Accusations from Medécins sans Frontières Christopher Lockyear, Secretary General of Medécins sans Frontières, declared on December 19, 2024, only three months into the war which Hamas had begun, that 'we are seeing clear signs of ethnic cleansing as Palestinians are forcibly displaced, trapped and bombed'. What he is describing is the Israeli notification to Gazan non-combatants to move out of the areas which they are going to bomb in the endeavour to defeat the Hamas terrorists. Is he suggesting that it would have been morally preferable not to suggest to civilians that they evacuate Hamas-occupied areas? Lockyear went on to assert: 'What our medical teams have witnessed on the ground throughout this conflict is consistent with the descriptions provided by an increasing number of legal experts and organisations concluding that genocide is taking place in Gaza'. It is by no means evident that Lockyear knows what the crime of genocide actually is. It does not mean the killing of children in the course of a legitimate war against an aggressor. It is defined in international law as an *intentional* crime. Hamas committed genocidal crimes, intending to kill, burn to death, and decapitate children, firing thousands of rockets indiscriminately onto Israeli cities and villages to kill civilians and children. Lockyear produced no evidence whatsoever that Israel deliberately aimed to kill innocent people and children, as opposed to killing Hamas terrorists. He refers to 'an increasing number of legal experts and organisations' without naming any. It seems that each NGO takes in the dirty washing from some other NGO.

Accusations from Danish Refugee Council The renowned Danish Refugee Council followed suit. Lila Thapa, the executive director for the Council in the Middle East, declared: 'This report exposes the systematic deprivation of basic necessities and forced displacement in Gaza, actions that could constitute violations under Article II of the Genocide Convention. These deliberate policies have trapped families in relentless cycles of suffering, denying them their fundamental rights under humanitarian rights law and International Humanitarian Law. The international community must act decisively to uphold international Humanitarian Law, deliver life-saving aid, and hold perpetrators accountable.' It is remarkable that the deprivers of basic necessities are not said to be Hamas, which seizes control of the aid lorries, but Israel, which – to repeat – has no obligation under international law to supply food or humanitarian aid or even to facilitate the supply of such aid *as long as it has serious reasons for fearing that the aid is being diverted from civilians to enemy military forces.* The perpetrators of the war in Gaza, according to the Danish Refugee Council, are not Hamas, which opened a savage, genocidal war against Israel and the Jews, but rather Israel, which was fighting a seven-front war to survive.

3. *Could all of these be wrong?* To the ill-informed bystander, could all these heads of NGOs be wrong? Could all these liberal progressive newspapers be mistaken? Could the BBC – 'The World's most trusted International News Broadcaster' or 'The World's Radio Station' as it announces its Overseas Service – be telling lies and distorting the truth? Could the governments of Europe be deluded? Could the United Nations and the Secretary General be falsifying the facts on a grand scale?

Compare all this with early Christian Church fathers' accusations against Jews The question is akin to the comparable question that might have been asked in the heyday of Byzantium. Are the Jews not evil deicides, the accursed of God? Do the Gospels not tell us that the Jews brought it all upon themselves by killing the son of God? Could the great St Paul be wrong? Could the Emperor and Empress be mistaken? Could Tertullian and St Jerome be telling us lies? Could St John Chrysostom be making it all up? That was surely unthinkable! But, for all that, the answer is: Yes, they were all wrong, in the most horrible and pernicious way. And millions of Jews ever since have been slaughtered, raped, and pillaged as a result. The ignorant claims of one respected authority are taken as established truths by another. Each false pronouncement is then cited as supporting evidence for another authority and a further allegation.

4. *Atrocity-crime reflection (mirror-imaging): origin of the 'bloody-hand' symbol* We have already noted the curious phenomenon of 'atrocity-crime reflection (mirror-imaging)'. Hamas, Hezbollah, and their Iranian masters are explicitly committed to and embarked on what was a genocidal slaughter of Jews, and yet it is the Jews who are condemned around the world and in the ICJ as well as the ICC, for committing genocide. A common sign of the evil Israelis in demonstrations in the Western and antipodean world has been the imprint of a bloody hand on the wall or on posters. Its origin is in the slaughter of two Israeli sergeants in a jeep at the time of the first intifada, who mistakenly took a wrong turning into Ramallah (then the headquarters of Arafat and the PLO) and stopped at a police station to ask for directions out of Ramallah. They were slaughtered and their killer, standing on a first-floor balcony, triumphantly raised his hands, dipped in their blood, to the mob below to celebrate the killing. But, perversely, this symbol is now being used to symbolize what is alleged to be an Israeli genocidal war.

5. *The accusation of genocide*: This accusation, as noted, is a novel form of blood libel: Hamas and Iran are ideologically committed to wiping Israel off the face of the earth and slaughtering its Jewish inhabitants, yet it is Israel that is accused of genocide. However, if Israel is committing genocide in the Gaza Strip, it is astonishingly inefficient about it: there were 200,000 Gazans living in the Gaza Strip after the end of the war in 1948 and there are two million today. The birth rate in Gaza is among the highest in the world. There are no gas chambers in the Gaza Strip, no industrialization of slaughter, and no sending of Palestinians from occupied territories in Lebanon or from Judaea and Samaria for gassing. Nor is there any policy of starvation. The innumerable food trucks that Israel allowed into the Gaza strip have contained enough food to supply each member of the population with 3,000 calories a day. If this did not reach all Gazans, that was because

the distribution was commandeered by Hamas, taxed, distributed to its active supporters and sold to others at inflated prices. Nor were Gazan children removed from their parents for purposes of re-education; on the contrary, Gazan children (and children in the West Bank) were educated by UNWRA, whose schoolbooks were antisemitic, glorifying jihad and terrorism. Elementary arithmetic was taught by means of such questions as 'If our heroic jihadists encounter seven Jews and kill five, how many Jews are left?'[2] Children's cartoons made for Gazan TV included such scenes as a tree telling heroic jihadist fighters that there is a Jew hiding behind it, who is then promptly killed.

6. *Left-wing selectivity in wrath* With the horrendous list of the numbers of the slaughtered in genocides since 1900, it is noteworthy that even accepting Hamas's Health Ministry's false figures of casualties in Gaza, there have been at most 48,000 killed (including terrorists) in a war started by Hamas, not by Israel. It is puzzling that demonstrations of 200,000 slogan-chanting anti-Zionists could be turned out on the streets of any Western capital on any weekend for months on end over the Gaza War, but no group of self-righteous left-wing activists is even tempted to demonstrate weekly for many consecutive months against the present Chinese regime over the destruction of Tibetan culture and Tibetan society, or over the million Uyghars maltreated and brainwashed in internment camps, or against the current Burmese (Myanmar) dictatorship and their genocidal war against the Rohingyas, in which some 900,000 Moslems have been forcibly evicted from Myanmar into Bangladesh since 2017, with extensive slaughter, rape, and burning of villages and towns.

M.C. Maguire (Irish Nobel laureate), Norwegian diplomat, Tom Pailin (Irish poet), Vatican spokesman: tunnel vision and bigotry It should, however, be noted, that this accusation is not new. Mairead Corrigan Maguire, Nobel Prize winner in 1977 for her attempts to bring peace to Northern Ireland, was enraged at the news that Israel had nuclear weapons: 'When I think about nuclear weapons, I've been to Auschwitz concentration camp ... Nuclear weapons are only gas chambers perfected ... and for a people who know what gas chambers are, how can you even think of building perfect gas chambers?'[3] In 2009, a senior Norwegian diplomat in Saudi Arabia sent an email from a Norwegian foreign ministry account, saying, 'The children of Holocaust survivors from the Second World War are doing to the Palestinians exactly what was done to them by Nazi Germany.'[4]

Northern Irish poet and academic Tom Paulin wrote a poem in *The Observer* on February 18, 2001, entitled 'Killed in Crossfire', apropos a Gazan boy's death in fighting in the Gaza Strip, 'another little Palestine boy … is gunned down by the Zionist SS'. In 2009, when Israel yet again launched a retaliatory attack on Hamas for its attacks on Israeli villages and towns, the Vatican Justice and Peace Minister Cardinal Renato Martino said, 'Defenceless populations are always the ones who pay. Look at the conditions in Gaza: more and more it resembles a big concentration camp.'[5] It was, it seems, even then, legitimate for Hamas indiscriminately to bombard Israeli towns, but if the Israelis retaliated, they were Nazis.

7. The African-American WOKE movement has been supporting the accusation of Israeli genocide in the Gaza war. It has also accused Israel of practising apartheid – an accusation advanced by the prominent Cameroonian theorist Achille Mbembe in 2020 who wrote that Israel's treatment of the Palestinians was far worse that the South African apartheid. The fact that Israeli Arabs (almost two million) have a free press, access to free primary, secondary and tertiary education, enjoy freedom of movement within Israel, participate in the independent judiciary and have had a seat on the Supreme Court, have equal suffrage in parliamentary elections to the Knesset and have representatives in the Knesset, have free access to an advanced national health system, receive child allowances, unemployment benefits and retirement pensions are, one must presume, just irrelevant facts as far as Mbembe is concerned. The condition of Arab Israelis is far from perfect and often needs improving. But they are not subject to apartheid.

If there is any apartheid in the Middle East and North Africa, it is in Muslim lands, where, since 1948, more than 800,000 Jews have been stripped of all their property and forcibly evicted from their ancestral homes – a figure greater than the 583,000 to 609,000 Palestinian Arabs who were refugees from Israel in the Israeli War of Independence in 1948.[6] The value of Jewish assets seized by Muslim nations and Iran is estimated by JJAC (Justice for Jews from Arab Nations) to be $59 billion at 2025 prices. The Jewish community in Egypt, estimated to have been between 75,000 and 80,000 in 1948, is now less than 20. The Moslem Middle East is in effect *Judenfrei*. Moreover, Mahmoud Abbas, President of the Palestinian Authority, now (2025) in the

twentieth year of his four-year term of elected office, strives to negotiate for a two-state solution, on condition that no Jews be allowed
within the projected Palestinian state. This will be discussed below.

8. *Settler-colonial studies in USA universities: the accusation of neo-
colonialism*: The accusation that Israel was a white neo-colonialist
state was especially prominent on American campuses. It has its roots
in the writings of Frantz Fanon (1925–61), a radical, neo-Marxist, political theorist, and in Soviet and post-Soviet Russian propaganda. The
doctrines of anti-neo-colonialism were produced in post-modernist
USA as an ideology about the USA, Canada, and Australia – all countries colonized by white European settlers on land taken away from
the indigenous people. Being a settler-colonialist is not argued to
be a status of those European white settlers prior to the independence of these colonies, which ceased once they became independent
states that accepted immigrants. Rather, it is asserted to be an inher-
itable identity irrespective of where one is born (hence even African
Americans are settler-colonialists according to this doctrine, and only
native American Indians are not). These doctrines were enthusiastically embraced by Muslims and by neo-Marxist academics in the USA
and harnessed to their anti-Zionist crusade. Yale professor Zareena
Grewal posted on X (Twitter) the declaration, 'Israel is a murderous,
genocidal settler state – Palestinians have every right to resist this
through armed struggle' (the Hamas genocidal attack on Israeli men,
women, children and babies being thus classified). Joseph Massad, a
Palestinian intellectual and professor at Columbia University described
the events of October 7 as a 'major achievement of the resistance in
the temporary take-over of these settler-colonies'. The Movement for
Black Lives sang the same tune, demanding 'an immediate end to
Israel's lethal settler-colonial Zionist apartheid'. The Salt Lake City
Chapter of Democratic Socialists of America urged all to 'stand up
against settler-colonial Zionist apartheid'.[7] Settler Colonial Studies is
now a flourishing academic discipline in American universities. The
incoherences and absurdities of this left-wing ideology have been well
described and exposed by Adam Kirsch and I shall not repeat them.
All I shall do is explain why the epithets 'colonial' and 'white colonial
settlers' have no application to the State of Israel and its inhabitants. The
State of Israel was not a colony of any imperial power. It was preceded
by a British Mandate (not a colony), established on the recommendation of the League of Nations, committed to providing a homeland for

the Jews after the First World War. Virtually all the Jewish inhabitants of the State of Israel are either refugees (from Russian pogroms and USSR antisemitism, European genocide and persecution, and Islamic ethnic cleansing throughout the Middle East and North Africa) or their descendants. None are colonialists in any legitimate sense of the word. The settlers in Judaea and Samaria might be said to be colonials in some sense, but not according to international law.

9. *UN resolution: 'Zionism is racism: the accusation of racism*: In 1975, the General Assembly of the UN, in a resolution sponsored by the Arab League and other Muslim countries, condemned Israel as a racist society ('Zionism is racism'). This was revoked only in 1991. It set the stage for the infamous Durban resolution in September 2001 at the World Conference against Racism in South Africa, authorized by the UN General Assembly (Res. 52/111). This was a huge conference of 1,500 NGOs with 5,000 delegates. The UN Human Rights Commission was the host organizer which held its preparatory planning conference in Teheran in July 2001. During the Durban conference, anti-Israel marches and demonstrations were supported by the South African NGOs linked to the Palestine Liberation Organization. They distributed antisemitic literature (including the infamous antisemitic *Protocols of the Elders of Zion*), T-shirts with a swastika imposed on the Star of David, placards reading 'If only Hitler had won'. The conference passed a resolution condemning Israel as a racist society. This resolution fuelled subsequent BDS (Boycott, Divest, and Sanction) campaigns in North America, Europe, and Australia. In 2021, the UN Human Rights Council planned a conference to celebrate the twentieth anniversary of the Durban resolution.

Racist anti-racism The accusation of racism is coupled to the idea that the Israelis are *white* colonials. This bizarre accusation seems to be a racist form of anti-racism. However, the majority of Jewish Israeli citizens are of North African and Middle Eastern origin, hence brown-skinned rather than white. Moreover, the dark-skinned Ethiopian Jews numbering more than 170,000, airlifted to Israel between the 1980s and 2021 in various waves to escape persecution, have been welcomed in Israel. Jews are a people, not a race.

10. *Accusations of violation of international law*: We have already noted the glibness with which NGOs accuse Israel of violating international law despite being ignorant of what international law does or does not require.

International law on collateral damage A common claim is that Israel violated international law in so far as its military response in the war against Hamas (which Israel did not start) is not proportional. Many confused people and journalists seem to think that if Hamas murdered hundreds of Israelis, then the IDF is entitled to kill only hundreds in retaliation. If it kills more, then that is a disproportionate response and contrary to international law. That is false. In international law, a military response against a warring party must not be in excess of what is necessary to achieve the legitimate goal of defeating the enemy. Israel is in compliance with international law if its actions are no more than what is necessary to destroy Hamas or force it to surrender.

A related claim is that Israel is in violation of international law if it kills innocent civilians. That too is false. Collateral damage is to be expected in warfare and is not in violation of international law. As already noted above, what *would* be illegal is the wilful killing of civilians for no military purpose (as was done by Hamas), or wilful killing of prisoners after they have given up their arms and surrendered (as was also done by Hamas).

No obligation in international law to supply electricity to Gaza, but Israel did Israel has been accused of violating international law in not supplying electricity to Gaza. But there is no obligation in international law to supply electricity to a warring enemy during wartime. I have found no example in the last hundred years when a country, responding to having been viciously attacked by an enemy, has proceeded to supply its attackers with electricity.

No obligation in international law to supply food to Gaza, but Israel did Israel has been accused of being in violation of international law in not supplying food aid to Gaza. Israel has no obligation to *supply* food aid to the citizens of Gaza. It does not even have an obligation to *facilitate* the supply of food and humanitarian aid, if it has reason to suspect that it will end up in the hands of its sworn enemy Hamas. But as has already been noted, that is precisely what happened. Nevertheless, Israel did persist in allowing 1.3 million tons of food aid to enter the Gaza Strip. Indeed, there was a surplus of assistance. Dividing the tonnage of food entering Gaza in the course of the war by the estimated number of Gazans yields the figure of 3,000 calories per person per day – considerably in excess of what is the desirable per capita food consumption according to the NHS of Britain. What is true is that Israel occasionally prevented a few lorries from entering Gaza if the lorries did not comply with the requirement that the goods be so loaded on flat trailers to enable examination by COGAT (Co-ordinator of Government Activities; the IDF unit responsible for facilitation of humanitarian aid and for checking such aid to ensure that no arms are being smuggled in).

11. *ICC under Karim Khan acted ultra vires* Israel has been condemned by the ICC for committing genocide and crimes against humanity, contrary to the requirements of international law. The ICC Prosecutor Karim Khan requested the issuing of arrest warrants against Israeli Prime Minister Benjamin Netanyahu and the Minister of Defence Yoav Galant for these crimes. However, he was arguably acting *ultra vires*. The Court has no jurisdiction to adjudicate on conflicts occurring on territories of countries that are not signatories to the Rome Treaty that set up the ICC in 1998 (endorsed by the General Assembly of the UN in December 1999 and again in December 2000) or to actions that have been filed by entities that are not member states of the Treaty. Israel is not a signatory since Arab countries insisted on including, on the list of war crimes the ICC may adjudicate, 'the action of transferring population into occupied territory' with the intention of targeting Israeli citizens. Palestine is not a sovereign state and so cannot file actions before the Court. The Security Council has not referred any case against Israel to the Court (any attempt to do so would have been vetoed by the USA). The Prosecutor, however, may initiate investigations on his own initiative (*proprio motu*). This is what Karim Khan did.

Karim Khan's illegal actions On May 20, 2024, Karim Khan issued a public statement at a press conference. His summary of the facts that allegedly warranted his initiative included allegations of intentional starvation and of deliberate targeting of civilians. The United Kingdom Lawyers for Israel organization, led by its distinguished legal director, Natasha Hausdorff, submitted documentation to the Prosecutor demonstrating that every single allegation was false. Rather than reviewing the evidence, Karim Khan instructed the Court to ignore any and all submissions on the question of accuracy of information that did not come from him. It was, therefore, on the basis of false information that Khan decided to issue warrants for the arrest of Netanyahu and Galant. Furthermore, since the ICC, unlike the ICJ, deals with individuals rather than with states, the only way the Court can try individuals for crimes allegedly committed in a certain territory is if the state with jurisdiction over that territory delegates it to the Court or accepts the Court's ad hoc jurisdiction over it. Israel, unsurprisingly, did not. But the Court decided that 'the State of Palestine' is sufficiently a state to be able to join the Court and delegate such jurisdiction. But Palestine is not a state in international law. The Palestinian authority under Mahmoud Abbas purports to have joined the Rome Statute (this being an aspect of its weaponization of international law against Israel). However, the criteria of statehood in international law are clearly laid out in the Montevideo Convention, and it is patent that the Palestinian Authority does not satisfy them. These criteria include a permanent population (as opposed to refugees); a defined territory (as opposed to the division of Judaea and Samaria (the 'West Bank') by the Oslo Accords into Areas A, B, and C, of which only Area A is under full control of the Palestinian Authority; and the ability in international law to enter into state relations.

12. *ICJ's abuse of power and international misinterpretation of its verdict* Israel has been brought before the ICJ in the Hague to answer accusations of committing genocide and crimes against humanity in the Gaza War. The ICJ is an organ of the UN, set up to adjudicate disputes between states. Its fifteen justices are elected by the General Assembly of the UN to serve for nine-year terms. It renders judgements by relative majority, and dissenting opinions are allowed. All member states of the UN may initiate contentious legal cases. In 2023, South Africa approached the Court for a decision on whether events in the war in Gaza could plausibly be raised as falling within its jurisdiction on acts of genocide and crimes against humanity. On January 26, 2024, the ICJ ruled that South Africa 'claimed "plausible rights"', i.e. had raised a case that engaged the Genocide Convention and therefore fell within the jurisdiction of the Court.[8] This decision was widely misinterpreted by the world's press and governments (and by the BBC) as condemning Israel for genocide – a misunderstanding enthusiastically encouraged by South Africa.

This egregious misinterpretation led to an Open Letter on April 3, 2024 (the first of a number of such public letters), signed by Lord Sumption and three other members of the English Supreme Court as well as some hundreds of other lawyers, addressed to the Prime Minister Rishi Sunak. It advised him that because of the condemnation of Israel by the ICJ, Britain had a legal obligation to impose sanctions on Israel and to stop all arms exports to it. This Open Letter was swiftly demonstrated to be both misconceived and misinformed by Natasha Hausdorff in her evidence to the Business and Trade Committee of the House of Commons on April 24, 2024. On April 25, Judge Joan Donoghue, a former president of the ICJ, who had herself authored the Provisional Measures Order, confirmed Natasha Hausdorff's analysis of the ICJ ruling.

It is remarkable that the ICJ President had been the Lebanese representative at the UN and had voted hundreds of times against Israel. In 2024, South Africa submitted an emergency request for the ICJ to order Israel to cease its Rafah offensive.[9] Subsequently, the ICJ President, Nawaf Salam,[10] declared on May 24, 2024, that 'The State of Israel shall immediately halt its military offensive, and any other action in the Rafah governate, which may inflict on the Palestinian group in Gaza conditions of life that could bring about its physical destruction in whole or in part'. The resolution was passed by a vote of 13 to 2, the dissenters being Israel itself and the Ugandan judge, Julia Sebutinde, who objected to the verdict's serious ambiguity, since it equivocates between ordering Israel to halt its war against Hamas (who had started the war), and ordering it to cease any actions in Gaza that may be genocidal – which it was not committing in the first place (this was akin to the spurious order to stop beating your wife, addressed to a man who was not beating his wife anyway.). It also disregarded the fact that Israel is not in sole control of the Rafah crossing, which it shares with Egypt, and made no mention of the fact that Israel had allowed a superfluity of food and humanitarian aid into Gaza.

So much for accusations of Israel's violating international law.

13. *Accusations of non-cooperation with Mahmoud Abbas*: Almost all political leaders in the West and in the antipodes, do not merely insist that there should be a ceasefire (leaving Hamas and Hezbollah in control), but also that the ceasefire should lead immediately to negotiations for a two-state solution that would resolve the conflict between Israel and the Palestinians. This would involve negotiations with the President of the Palestinian Authority, Mahmoud Abbas. As will now be shown, it is doubtful whether he is a person with whom any binding negotiations for a peace agreement can be held.

Mahmoud Abbas: personal record Abbas, born in 1935 in Safed, fled with his family to Damascus in 1948. He studied law at the University of Damascus and did his doctorate at the Patrice Lumumba University in Moscow in the department of Zionology. His doctorate was entitled 'The Other Side: the Secret Relationship between Nazism and Zionism'. In it he argued that Zionists were 'fundamental partners' in the Nazi Holocaust, collaborating in killing large numbers of Jews, in order to encourage the rest to emigrate to Palestine. He alleged that the Eichmann abduction and trial were a cover up to prevent Eichmann from revealing to *Life* magazine the Zionist involvement in the Holocaust. He asserted that the numbers of Jews murdered in the Holocaust was grossly exaggerated by Jews, since only 890,000, not 6 million, were murdered. The propagation of gross historical falsehoods, it seems, became second nature, since in a speech to the Fatah Revolutionary Council in August 2023, Abbas asserted that Ashkenazi Jews are not descendants of any Jews in ancient Judaea, but were all descendants of Khazar converts, so lacking any historical connection with Palestine.

Abbas and Fatah (PLO) Abbas was a founding member of Fatah in the late 1950s. He became the primary international negotiator for the PLO, presenting a moderate face of a terrorist organization to the world. In 1977, he called for the repatriation of all 'Arab Jews' to their countries of origin in North Africa and the Middle East. In this he was merely repeating the declaration of the first leader of the PLO, Ahmed Shukeiry, in 1967, luxuriating in the expected triumph of Nasser in late May 1967. In 1993, he was chief Palestinian negotiator and signatory at the Oslo Accords. However, he viewed the 'peace process' as the continuation of the strife with Israel by other means. As late as July 2002, he described Oslo as 'the biggest mistake Israel ever made', since it gave the PLO world-wide legitimacy as representative of the Palestinian people, without abandoning its commitments, in particular the right of return. Shortly after Arafat's death in November 2004, Abbas, in his address to the Palestinian Legislative Council, swore to 'follow in the path of the late leader Yasir Arafat and … work toward fulfilling his dream. … We promise you that our hearts will not rest until the right of return for our people is achieved and the tragedy of the refugees ended'. To be sure, the right of return is a euphemism for the end of the Jewish State of Israel. When Ehud Olmert, Prime Minister of Israel 2006–9, at the US sponsored peace talks at Annapolis, Md. (Maryland, USA), offered Abbas a Palestinian Arab state on 97% of the 'West Bank' together with the Gaza Strip and with its capital in east Jerusalem, Abbas rejected the offer, insisting on the right of return. In April 2009, when Netanyahu, newly elected prime minister, asked for Abbas's recognition of Israel as a Jewish state, Abbas responded, 'A Jewish state, what does that supposed to mean [*sic*!]? You can call yourselves as you like, but I don't accept it and I say so publicly.' At Fatah's 6th general congress in August 2009, Abbas affirmed its armed struggle, which 'will not stop until the Zionist entity is eliminated, and Palestine is liberated'.

Abbas's corruption Abbas's regime, like Arafat's before him, has been characterized by corruption. Arafat was reported by one of his close aides Mohammed Rashid, as having siphoned off nearly a billion US dollars to his own bank accounts (duly inherited by his widow and children). Abbas, according to Rashid, was more modest, having a mere hundred million.

Abbas's 'Pay for Slay' policy Abbas was in charge of payments to families of terrorists ('Foundation for the Care of Martyrs'), and payments to convicted and imprisoned terrorists ('Martyrs' Fund', referred to by Israelis as the 'Pay for Slay' Fund), many of whom are murderers or mass-murderers. These funds are administered by the PLO, with a bureaucracy of 500 Palestinians. They pay out $300 million a year. When Western powers objected to payments for murder, Abbas responded indignantly that such interference was an 'aggression against the Palestinian people' and insisted that salaries for imprisoned Palestinians was a 'social responsibility'. When, on January 30, 2025, Israel released 734 terrorists (including 200 convicted murderers) in exchange for 33 Israeli hostages, the released terrorists had received reward salaries totalling $141 million, quite apart from payments to wives and families.

Mahmoud Abbas is 89 years old and unlikely to live through the consequences of any negotiations. No one knows what the Palestinian Authority will look like after his death. That alone disqualifies him as a plausible signatory for any peace agreement, were one on the horizon. Moreover, given his record of deception, corruption, and dishonesty, he is wholly untrustworthy. His conception of truth is purely pragmatic: only speak truly when the truth is in your interest.

14. *Accusations of rejection of a two-state solution* Let us now turn to the proposal of a two-state solution to the conflict between the Arab Palestinians and the Israelis. There are four salient points to be made concerning this suggestion.

Two-state solutions have always been rejected by Arab Palestinian leaders. First, the Palestinians were offered a state in a part of the British Mandated territory or on the 'West Bank' of the Kingdom of Jordan, numerous times, and turned it down each time.

Peel Commission Partition Plan 1937 rejected by Arab Palestinian leaders The Peel Commission Partition Plan in 1937, set up to establish the causes of the 1936 Arab revolt led by Amin Husseini, the Mufti of Jerusalem, and to recommend how peace could be restored, recommended abandonment of the terms of the British Mandate to set up a National Home for the Jews, in favour of partition. It recommended an Arab state, to be united with the Kingdom of Transjordan, that would incorporate 85% of the mandated territory, and a Jewish state in the remaining 15% (see Map 6). Jerusalem, Bethlehem, and a connecting corridor to the Mediterranean were to remain a British zone. The commission recommended a land and population exchange between the two communities on the model of the Greek/Turkey settlement in 1922. The recommendation was immensely disadvantageous to the Jews, overwhelmingly favourable to the Arabs. With the gravest of foreboding, the Jews accepted partition but rejected the minute allocation of land to a Jewish state. King Abdullah of Transjordan accepted the plan with alacrity. The Mufti of Jerusalem, the Arab Higher Committee, and the Arab states rejected it out of hand.

A second occasion on which the Arab Palestinians were offered an Arab state in part of what was mandated Palestine was in 1947. On November 29, 1947, the General Assembly of the UN voted for the partition of Palestine into a Jewish state and an Arab state linked in an economic union, with Jerusalem placed under the UN control (see Map 6). The immediate response in Palestine was an outbreak of murderous violence that persisted until the British withdrew and the War of Independence established the existence of the State of Israel as a fact on the ground, so to speak (as opposed to the declaration of the General Assembly of the UN, which is not in fact empowered to create states).

During the Israel War of Independence 1947–8, the Kingdom of Transjordan conquered what became known as the 'West Bank'. The armistice lines in 1949 ran around this territory, leaving Israel a mere 12 miles wide between Haifa and Tel Aviv (see Map 7). These were never intended to be permanent boundaries. The armistice was meant to be a prelude to negotiations for a final settlement and peace. But the Arab states that had attacked Israel were unwilling to enter into negotiations and remained in a state of war with the nascent state (in accordance with the principle of *hudna*). The Palestinians, and their leaders, had placed their faith in the Arab states and their victory, little realizing that none of the Arab states had the slightest concern for the Palestinian Arabs but were motivated only by the desire to destroy Israel and to grab what land they could. Transjordan formally annexed the West Bank in 1950.

Successive offers of a Palestinian state in Judaea and Samaria ('West Bank') were rejected There were various attempts under American aegis to negotiate a peace settlement with the Palestinian Arabs, whose official representative had been recognized in the Oslo Accords (1993) to be the Palestine Liberation Organization led by the terrorist leader Yasser Arafat (1929–2004). In 2000, at Camp David, Ehud Barak offered Arafat an independent Palestinian state in Gaza and 90% of the West Bank with east Jerusalem (but not the Old City) as its capital. As President Clinton later said, 'Arafat was here for 14 days and said No to everything.' In 2007/8, Ehud Olmert negotiated with Mahmoud Abbas in Annapolis, Md., under the aegis of President Bush, and increased Barak's offer to 97% of the West Bank, allowing repatriation of Palestinians with relatives in Israel, and generous compensation for others. Abbas turned this down. It is evident that Abbas, as he himself insisted in his speeches to Palestinian political bodies, was carrying on the policies of his predecessor Arafat. His goal has never been anything other than the eradication of the State of Israel. The Palestinian Arabs have been unfortunate in their leaders, from Husseini, through Arafat, to Abbas. As Abba Eban, Israel's foreign minister and representative in the UN, once said, 'They never missed an opportunity to miss an opportunity'. Fixated on the destruction of Israel, they were unwilling to face the simple fact that Israel was there to stay. They had no qualms in sacrificing the welfare of their own people in the single-minded pursuit of their goal and their personal domination.

Second, the Palestinian population of Judaea and Samaria do not want any such solution. They wanted a one-state solution – that state being an Arab one, with Jews descended from Jewish Palestinians in 1948 allowed to remain as second-class citizens, and the others returned to their or their parents' countries of origin. 72% of Palestinians in the 'West Bank' applauded the October 7 massacres.

Third, if there were an election in the proposed new Palestinian state on the 'West Bank', there would be one and only one election, in which Hamas would replace the Palestinian Authority.

Fourth, what would such a state look like? Would it have its own independent armed forces? These would undoubtedly be armed to the teeth by Iran (or by Turkey?). Would it be an autonomous state capable of entering into treaties with other states? – if so, what would prevent it from signing a mutual security pact with Iran and inviting Iranian armed forces to move in? Would it control the heights overlooking the Jordan valley and indeed the Jordan valley itself – both essential for Israeli security in these days of drone and rocket warfare? It would almost certainly want to take over the Kingdom of Jordan that already has a swollen Palestinian population. Is that a desirable outcome from any point of view?

It may be that there was once a time in which it made political and moral sense for there to be a liberal-democratic state on the 'West Bank', but that time has long since passed. The Palestinians don't want it and never have. It is impossible that there be anything like a Palestinian *liberal-democratic state* in as much as the social institutions and socio-political mentality essential for a liberal democracy to exist do not obtain among the Palestinians any more than among any of the Arab states. Israel is the one and only liberal democracy in the Middle East, and, unfortunately, an increasingly precarious one under the leadership of Netanyahu and his right-wing reactionary government. The Israelis have good reasons to think that a Palestinian state would be national suicide for Israel in present circumstances. There *is* no two-state solution, for the 'two-state solution' is not a solution *at the present time*. Equally certainly, the two peoples must, *sometime*, learn to live together in peace between the river and the sea.

Notes

1 She had previously distinguished herself by tweeting in January 2013 that Shimon Peres had admitted in a *New York Times* interview that Yasser Arafat had been murdered by Israelis. This was nothing other than malicious fiction. In April 2021, Amnesty International released a statement that the tweet did not reflect the position of Amnesty International or of Callamard.

2 See Georg Eckert Institute for International Textbook Research *Report on Palestinian Textbooks* 2021.urn:nbn:de:0220-2021-0020. Furthermore, in July 2024, the EU allocated 400 million Euros in grants and loans to

the Palestinian Authority for schoolbooks in the Gaza Strip, subject to progress in implementing reforms agreed upon by the Gaza educational authorities to eliminate antisemitic material and incitement to violence and jihad. No such reforms occurred. In September 2024, Abdul Hakim Abu Jamous, a senior educational official told the Palestinian newspaper *Al Quds* that Ramallah had never agreed to EU demands on educational change (although by then the EU had already provided the promised funding). In a report issued on March 27, 2025, IMPACT (Institute for Monitoring Peace and Cultural Tolerance, an Israeli/UK based watchdog) announced that new Gazan online textbooks continue to glorify jihadist martyrs, include commentary on the Quran portraying Jews as liars and deceivers, and continue to teach arithmetic with examples of numbers of heroic jihadi martyrs per week. In Khan Younis Al-Safa wal-Marwa School, pupils staged a dance to a song glorifying resistance with gestures by the early-teen girls mimicking throats being cut (video online).

3 'Nobel Peace Laureate compares Israel to Nazi Germany', Associated Press, December 19, 2004.

4 Etgar Lefkovits, 'Norwegian envoy: Israel, Nazis the same', *Jerusalem Post*, January 21, 2009.

5 'Gaza resembles concentration camp', *Jerusalem Post*, January 8, 2009.

6 Figures calculated on the basis of British Mandate figures by Efraim Karsh, *Palestine Betrayed* (Yale University Press, New Haven, 2010), Appendix.

7 All quotations from Adam Kirsch, *On Settler Colonialism: Ideology, Violence, and Justice* (W. W. Norton, 2024).

8 It was subsequently shown that the quotations that South Africa presented to the Court as Israeli 'incitements to genocide' were quotations removed from their original context, in which they referred to Hamas atrocities, not to Israel's intentions.

9 It is curious that South Africa has been so prominent in anti-Israel 'lawfare' and so keen to get Israel condemned in international forums. It has spent substantial sums of money on its anti-Zionist propaganda and its submissions to the ICJ. This requires further investigation.

10 The presiding President of the Court, Nawaf Salam should have recused himself since he was Lebanese and prior to his appointment to the Court on February 6, 2018, he was the Ambassador and Permanent Representative of Lebanon at the UN from 2007 to 2017, and had lent his voice and vote to hundreds of anti-Israel motions in the General Assembly and its committees. He is now prime minister of Lebanon.

7 Explaining the Public and the Student Responses

1. *The need to explain left-wing antisemitism* One purpose of this discussion was to explain the quite unprecedented response to the Gaza War and to Israel's conduct of the war that has been manifested throughout the Western World. Anti-Zionism, as has been shown, became a new transmutation of antisemitism, altogether unlike previous right-wing Fascist antisemitism. Moreover, it had a distinctive appeal to people under the age of 35, who conceived of themselves as 'liberal', 'progressive', or 'left-wing', and to university students. This was peculiar and calls out for explanation. Any explanation is bound to be manifold – there is no single, all-encompassing explanation. It is helpful to contextualize the widespread response. It is noteworthy that the Gaza War happened to coincide with:

(a) a psychological crisis in the Western World
(b) a demographic crisis
(c) a cultural crisis.

These provide the background *Zeitgeist* or 'spirit of the times' that informs the 2020s.

2. *The Gaza War coincided with a psychological crisis in the West* (a) The psychological crisis consists of the emergence and weaponization of identity politics that placed inordinate emphasis on the variety of group classifications that may be applied to any individual person, especially with regard to discrimination perceived to be disadvantageous. Critical Race Theorists introduced the notion of *intersectionality* according to which any member of any social group whose self-conception includes the idea that they are being

DOI: 10.4324/9781003711957-7

discriminated against should not think of themselves as an individual person with an array of problems that need to be confronted. Rather, they should think of themselves as having an overlapping set of identities, e.g. of sex, gender, race, religion, etc. The psychological crisis in the Western World has at least two distinct components: a cult of victimhood and a preoccupation with 'politically correct' speech, which has infiltrated not only schools, but also universities.

3. *The Glorification of victimhood* The cult and glorification of victimhood seems unprecedented in Western civilization. Its closest analogue is the martyrological cult among early Christians persecuted by Nero, Decius, Trebonius Gallus, and Diocletian prior to Constantine's declaring Christianity the official religion of the Empire. It seems plausible to link the current cult of victimhood to the post-Millennials' addiction to mass media, smartphones, and twittering.[1] These are conducive to narcissism, vulnerability, and anxiety. They are also inimical to reasoned debate. Rather, they demand mass consensus, on the one hand, and animus towards those who disagree, on the other.

4. *Political correctness* Political correctness affects politicians, the press, television, and radio in the UK, the USA, Canada, and Australia. It is engendering thought-policing for fear of offending anyone. Universities required their lecturers to declare whether the subject of their lecture might be found upsetting by someone in the audience. Paradoxically, university tolerance for free debate and diversity of opinion evaporated at the same time as rampant anti-Zionism was allowed to flourish in universities, being presented as 'free speech' rather than as antisemitism. Sometimes political correctness reached farcical heights. Nottingham University changed the description of some of its history and literature courses for undergraduates from 'Anglo-Saxon literature' and 'Anglo-Saxon history' to 'Early Medieval literature' and 'Early Medieval history' on the grounds that the expression 'Anglo-Saxon' is a racist supremacist epithet (especially in the USA) and suggests native Englishness. Nottingham, one might naively suppose, must be an American university.

5. *Demographic crisis in the West* The demographic crisis consists in the Islamization of the West. According to the World Population Review (figures for 2021), France has 5 to 6 million Muslims, Germany 4.6 million, UK 3.86 million, Spain 1.18 million, the USA 4 million, Canada 1.8 million. This population, especially when concentrated in

specific cities, constitutes an important electoral asset for politicians in general elections. Many politicians are therefore prone to cultivate the favour of their electors, in particular with regard to the Gaza War. Multi-culturalism is a much-favoured ideology of the political left. It is also a powerful centrifugal force undermining the cultural identity of nations. This in turn breeds the revival of right-wing fascism, as is evident in Germany, Austria, France, Holland, and Italy, and may well occur in Britain if there is a turn towards Nigel Farage and his Reform UK party.

6. *Cultural crisis of confidence* There is a cultural crisis in the West, particularly evident and cultivated in universities and among the educated elites: it is a crisis of confidence in Western culture. It has become a leitmotiv of university lecturers in the humanities and social sciences to denigrate Western art and science. Even such a luminary as Nobel Prize laureate Amartya Sen has contended that democracy 'is not a quintessentially Western idea, an immaculate Western conception'. He was definitively refuted by Paul Cartledge, professor of Greek Culture at the University of Cambridge.[2] It is common to present great Western ideas as originating in non-Western cultures (which many do), to argue that Western culture is the product of white male elites (which it largely is), and to denigrate the cultural and scientific achievement of the West (which is absurd). This breeds a pernicious lack of confidence in, and a hatred and contempt for our own civilization, coupled with intense, narcissistic, self-satisfaction and self-righteousness. Such ideas are profoundly destabilizing, undermining one of the integrative forces in society. Multi-culturalism is a socially centrifugal force.

7. *Need to explain left-wing antisemitism* It is against this context that we can explain the emergence of left-wing antisemitism in the guise of anti-Zionism. We are sadly familiar with right-wing, Fascist antisemitism, but antisemitism of the self-styled 'Progressive' left is novel. The fact that hundreds of universities and tens of thousands of university students were demonstrating on campuses and in encampments in the streets is curious. Why should the young, who have the privilege of a higher education, side with, demonstrate in support of, a genocidal death-cult like Hamas,[3] and against Israel, the only democracy in the Middle East? And why should criticism of the Israel government be transformed into anti-Zionism and blatant antisemitism? There are many reasons, woven together in a distinctive pattern.

8. *Neo-Marxist ideology* First: ideologies that explicitly or implicitly inform left-wing or progressive thought, in particular neo-Marxism. Marxism is an ideology that divides mankind into the oppressors and the oppressed. Students may know little if anything about Marxism. But given the cultural milieu of sanctification of victimhood, the thought that the Palestinians in the Gaza Strip are the oppressed victims of Israel's overwhelmingly powerful military is an easily assimilable simplification of a complex history.

9. *University students and post-modernism* Second: university students in particular, and the more or less educated classes in general, are prone to be persuaded by post-modernism. One (indefensible) doctrine of post-modernism is the denial of objective truth. There is only your truth and my truth – and both are equally valid. Hence the adoption of the idea that to each person and to each social group there corresponds a different 'narrative', all equally valid. This preconception disinclines progressives from judging the radical ideology and religion of Hamas. At best, they will be prone to condemn both Hamas and Israel indifferently.

Incoherence of relativization of truth To be sure, this is incoherent. It is obvious that the principle of the relativity of truth may be applied to itself. Is the contention that there is no objective truth itself an objective truth or is it too merely relative? To say that a given proposition is true is no more than to say that things are as the assertion of the propositions say they are. To go on to claim that we can never *know* whether any proposition is true or false would be an absurd form of scepticism. The relativist doctrine is a distortion of the obvious fact that we all have a large battery of background beliefs which provides the framework within which we view and come to terms with the reality we face. This is something we should be aware of, and we should be willing, occasionally, to question some of these beliefs and to judge their validity.

It should be clear that there is no ground for not condemning the principles of Hamas's ideology without qualification. Nor is there any good reason for adopting anti-Zionism, the denial of the right of the Jewish people to have a state of their own.

10. *Romantic cult of noble savage (Rousseau)* Third: among many self-styled progressives and among many students, there is a streak of romanticism – sympathy with ideas that were espoused by Rousseau (whether they have even heard of Rousseau is irrelevant). It is the romantic conception of noble savages, uncorrupted by modern society and modern civilization, untarnished by capitalism and post-capitalism.[4] This is readily linked to Tolstoyan ideas about the noble *muzhik*, whose simplicity of moral vision is superior to the reflections of civilized man and of corrupted Western civilization. It is easy to cast Palestinians, Hamas, and Islamic jihadists in the role of the heroic oppressed peasants fighting for freedom. To be sure, this involves averting one's gaze from their genocidal intent, the desire of Hamas (being offshoots of the Muslim Brotherhood) to impose Sharia law on any territory they may gain, their oppression of women, and their death-cult. A similar romanticism was true of the progressive left, two generations ago, in the adulation of Che Guevara.

11. *Blinkered revulsion at Western imperialism* A fourth factor, which we have mentioned in the previous discussion, is the anti-colonial, anti-imperialist ideology that is linked to a peculiar form of anti-racist racism. There is widespread condemnation of imperialism, which is associated with white peoples. In a *trahison des clercs* that is remarkable, academics are commonly given to wholesale condemnation of everything to do with imperialism and to associate imperialism with white Europeans. To be sure, this involves total disregard of non-western (non-white) imperialism (e.g. Arab imperialism in the eighth and ninth century spreading through the whole of the Middle East, Central Asia, and North Africa; Mongol imperialism; Moghul imperialism in India; Ottoman imperialism in the Middle East, the Balkans, and North Africa). It assumes that the conditions of the societies and peoples who were subjected to imperial rule by Western countries was one of blissful noble savagery. In at least some cases, the savagery was neither blissful nor noble. The imperial legacy was by no means uniformly bad. Modern medicine was brought to countries that knew nothing of it. Modern education and literacy were introduced to countries that lacked education altogether or whose only education was rooted in a stultifying past. Modern science and technology were extended to imperial colonies. Savage and barbaric customs were suppressed, such as the Hindu Indian practice of suttee. As for Jews being *white* colonials, as we have seen, it was falsely assumed that the Jews are a white people, whereas in fact the majority of Israelis are of Sephardic-Jewish ancestry. As for Jewish immigrants to the British Mandate and subsequently to Israel being *colonials*, they were refugees from persecution not only at the hands of Western colonial nations, but from persecution among the Muslim Powers of North Africa and the Middle East.

12. *Instinctive pacifism* Fifth: pacifism among the young and among the older generation. Unused to warfare on their doorsteps and unaccustomed to the relentless barrage of broadcasting on the Gazan War, there was a perfectly intelligible reaction of horror at the fact that so many people, in particular so many children (irrespective of Hamas's faked figures), were being killed. As government ministers are prone to say, when they have nothing helpful to say: 'It is completely unacceptable' and as members of the public, youthful and old, expressed their sentiments: 'It shouldn't be allowed'. But what was the alternative? That the Israelis 'turn the other cheek'? – and be subjected to further such massacres? That they sit down and negotiate for a two-state solution? – with Hamas, who are wholly committed to the destruction of Israel? With the Palestinian authority? – *that* had been tried more than once and failed. Moreover, how would it help in the Gaza Strip, which was ruled by Hamas?

13. *Anti-parental rebellion* Sixth: a characteristic feature of students and young people in general is a desire to rebel against the opinions of their parents and against what they perceive as the establishment view. The more radical the cause they embrace, the more exciting it is for them to shock their elders. Once embarked upon the chosen cause, they derive much reinforcing satisfaction from the camaraderie of their peers, on the one hand, and self-righteousness on the other. It feels good to think that one is on the right side of history. This familiar social phenomenon is an instance of the pleasure of the conformity of non-conformism, especially in crowd demonstrations and sit-ins.

14. *Passion for self-righteousness* Seventh: there is perhaps a darker side to the new transmutation of antisemitism in the guise of anti-Zionism. It is plausible to see a cultural shift in recent years towards expressing concealed, vicious passions under the cover of open, virtuous passions. I was myself struck by the remarks made by one of the 42 signatories to the Oxford Academics' *Open Letter on the Humanitarian Crisis in Gaza* that was addressed to the British Prime Minister Rishi Sunak and to the Leader of the Opposition Keir Starmer, in late October, 2023. She explained that when she heard of the Hamas massacre, she immediately went to see a Jewish friend and wept on her shoulder. This appeared to her to validate her Open Letter, which condemned Israel's war against Hamas as a 'morally disastrous exercise', 'an unprecedented human catastrophe', 'an affront to

basic moral dignity', and the imposition of 'collective punishment' on Gazans. This vicious condemnation of Israel is concealed by the pretext of defending the supposedly vulnerable Palestinians (who voted Hamas into office as their legitimate government), and the dark passion for gaining the moral high ground and for self-righteousness, concealed by the pretext of remedying supposed injustice.

These conjunctively render intelligible the reactions to the Gazan War among the youth and among those who conceive of themselves as 'progressive'. It has by no means ceased, any more than has the war. But in its seven-front war, Israel has transformed the political landscape in the Middle East. The Asad regime has been destroyed. Hezbollah has been largely destroyed, although whether the Lebanese will be able, at long last to take control of their own country is still unclear. Hamas has been largely destroyed, but it is still in partial control of the Gaza Strip. The Houthis have been severely hammered by the USA and are being hammered by Israel, although with what long term effect is unclear. The power of Iran to fight a proxy war and to achieve regional super-power status has been eliminated, but it is still a major regional actor and is still in pursuit of nuclear weapons.

Israel has paid sorely for an existential seven-front war, from which it has emerged victorious. But it is still ruled by the most reactionary and corrupt government it has ever had and still led by a prime minister who puts his own interests ahead of those of the country. The Palestinian condition on the West Bank remains as unresolved as ever, with little immediate hopes of resolution. The future of the Gaza Strip remains undetermined.

Notes

1 For extensive investigation of the psychological harm caused by smartphones and internet addiction among teenagers of the post-millennial generation, see Jonathan Heidt, *The Anxious Generation* (Penguin Randon House, UK, 2025).

2 See Paul Cartledge, *Democracy – A Life* (Oxford University Press, Oxford, 2016).

3 It is a death-cult in so far as it glorifies death in Holy War (*jihad*) and sanctifies *shahids* (those who are killed in a Holy War), who go straight to Heaven and whose sacrifice ensures that up to 70 members of their family will also go to Heaven.

4 It should be remarked that this romantic streak is also to be found among people who are in no sense disposed to left-wing ideas, e.g. T. E. Lawrence and Wilfred Thesiger.

8 Addendum

The Response to the Israel–Iran War

1. *Israel's response to Iran's attack* In the course of the war that began with the Hamas massacre of Israelis on October 7, 2023, Iran fought a war against what their leaders called 'the Zionist entity' by means of proxies: Hamas in the Gaza Strip, Hezbollah in Lebanon, Assad in Syria (whose cooperation was essential for the arming and supply of arms to Hezbollah), Islamic Jihad on the West Bank, the Houthis in Yemen, and sundry terrorist groups in Iraq (see Map 8). The Iranians only joined in active military engagement twice, when they launched hundreds of drones and ballistic missiles against Israel, most of which were shot down by the Israelis and the American naval forces in the area. The Israelis would have had every reason and justification for directly attacking Iran, but they were ordered not to do so by the Americans. It was only in June 2025 that this American order was countermanded by Donald Trump. On June 13, 2025 Israel launched surprise attacks on key military, governmental and nuclear facilities and leaders in Iran. Iran retaliated with waves of missile and drone strikes against Israeli cities, indiscriminably bombing civilians. On the 9th day the US joined Israel by bombing three Iranian nuclear sites, destroying or setting back a large part of Iran's endeavour to manufacture nuclear bombs. On the twelfth day of this war, Israel (reluctantly, since it had not finished the job) and Iran (with obvious relief) agreed to a ceasefire after pressure from America.

2. *Antisemitic reactions to Israel's self-defence* The usual pro-Palestinian, anti-Zionist groups ranted against 'the treacherous Zionist American aggressions' or posted on X antisemitic comparisons of Israel to Nazi Germany. Mirah Wood, a former leader of multiple subcommittees for the Democratic Socialists of America, wrote on

DOI: 10.4324/9781003711957-8

X: 'the world stands with iran, death to the israeli nazis and all their evil allies.'[1]

Meanwhile, the traditional antisemitic groups of the hard right responded to the Iran strikes by explicitly blaming 'the Jews' for starting a   third World War and wishing violence upon Israel. Antisemitic X account Gentile News Network posted: 'Jews are dragging us into another war again.' Another antisemitic X influencer, Red Pill Media, commented: 'Crypto is crashing because Israel struck Iran. You can blame Jews for that too.' Many of the white supremacist groups went far further.

3. *Iran's war guilt* Western governments' reactions were more oblique. Israel argued that its war was a response to the Islamic Republic's long affirmed intention to wipe Israel ('the Zionist entity') off the face of the world, and to the Iranian imminent production of a nuclear weapon. The day before the war began the IAEA had passed a resolution that declared Iran non-compliant with its nuclear obligations. Moreover, it was patent that Iran had backed the October 7 attacks and had conducted the subsequent war through its proxies. In the international response to the war, it was harder to represent Israel as the villain than it had been in the Gaza War. Since its inception The Islamic Republic has engaged in international terrorism, and created, trained and armed radical proxy groups across the region. Although Biden's administration was initially agnostic on the Iran-Hamas links, evidence has now emerged showing The Revolutionary Guard's funding and training of Hamas for the October 7 attacks.[2] Moreover it is widely understood that Iran's support of Hamas, Hezbollah, Assad, the Houthis, the Iraqi militias and other radical groups across the region contributed to the wider Middle Eastern crisis that followed October 7.

4. *West calls for Israeli restraint in self-defence* Despite this, few openly supported Israel's right to weaken and contain Iran with force. The message from most European leaders was that Israel was desta-bilizing the Middle East. In the UK, Starmer stated that he preferred a 'diplomatic approach', calling for 'restraint, calm and a return to diplomacy'[3]. The Dutch government found the war 'alarming' and called for 'restraint' from Israel.[4] Macron in France said that the US strikes were illegal and also called for diplomacy.[5] This was all des-pite decades of diplomacy that had failed to reassure anyone that Iran was abandoning its nuclear weapons program. Western governments,

afraid of Muslim opinion among their electorate and concerned about disruption of oil supplies and rises in the cost of oil, were keen to urge Israel not to defend itself against military threats to its existence. Merz in Germany alone stood out for praising the Israeli military for doing the 'dirty work' of attacking Iran.[6]

5. *BBC and NPR anti-Israeli reportage* Reporters who have been unsympathetic towards Israel throughout the conflict with Hamas, were now unsure whether they could bring themselves to support Iran's intention to develop nuclear weapons in order to annihilate Israel. Simon Plosker, editorial director of Honest Reporting (a US charity that reports on anti-Israeli bias) argued that coverage was better than the reporting on the conflict with Hamas.[7] But critical problems remained. Media outlets equated Israel's targeted military operations with Iran's indiscriminate missile attacks on civilians. The BBC radio's satirical programme, *Dead Ringers*, lampooned Israel's protest over Iran bombing its hospitals. It played an explosion; 'sorry that wasn't a missile that was the world's irony meter exploding'[8]; a joke of poor taste premised on the assumption that Israel also targeted hospitals, disregarding the fact that those hospitals were terrorist centres and command-and-control posts. After the ceasefire took effect on June 24, 2025, National Public Radio in the US equated Iran's killing Israeli civilians in their bomb shelters with Israel's strike on Iran's repressive Basij paramilitary militia. For NPR, both sides had simply 'exchanged attacks up to the final moments.'[9]

6. *Press bias* Second, many media outlets assumed that the US had no reason to get involved; this was Israel's war. When Israel attacked Iran, *The Guardian* wrote, 'Israel's strikes on Iran show Trump is unable to restrain Netanyahu as Middle East slips closer to chaos... The unilateral strikes indicated a collapse of Donald Trump's efforts to restrain the Israeli prime minister.' After the US bombing of Iran, the *New York Times* ran the headline: 'With Decision to Bomb Iran, Trump Injects U.S. Into Middle East Conflict; the United States has joined Israel's war against the country.'[10] *The Associated Press* head-line was no better: 'US Inserts Itself into War between Israel and Iran.' The BBC credited Netanyahu with 'changing the mind of a US presi-dent who campaigned against overseas military adventures.'[11] Such comments ignore America's own reasons for going to war and for supporting Israel, namely the long history of Iranian aggression dir-ectly against 'The Great Satan', from the Beirut bombings in 1983

to the attempt to assassinate Donald Trump last year, as well as its pivotal role in turning the Iraq War into the fiasco it became. Not only does this type of reporting stoke resentment against Israel and foster the myth of a global Jewish cabal influencing Washington, but it underplays the importance to the West of stopping the current Iranian regime becoming a Middle Eastern superpower, let alone getting nuclear weapons. It also ignores the fact that Trump vowed throughout his presidential campaign that he would do what was necessary to stop Iran's nuclearization.

7. *Humanizing Khamenei* Third, many publications attempted to humanize Khamenei, downplaying his role in causing the war. An essay in *The Conversation* fails to mention his establishment and support of terror proxies but finds space to mention his 'rare' literary interests and 'his interest in gardening'.[12] *The Economist,* in its profile of Khamenei, depicts how he was one of eight children born to a 'poor religious scholar from the north-east of Iran'. We're told he studied the Koran, 'listened to music, recited poetry and read novels such as *Les Misérables and The Grapes of Wrath'–* books that, *The Economist* implies, resonated with Khamenei because they 'depict secular struggles against oppression'. His own murderous, brutal oppression of his citizens is downplayed. There is no mention of his role in turning Iran into the world's foremost state sponsor of terror, funding groups like Hamas, Hezbollah, and the Houthis.[13]

8. *UK press misrepresentation of Netanyahu* Fourth, 'Argue the man, not the policy' may be a well-known debating tactic, but it is not one that reputable, unbiased media should deploy. Yet the BBC portrays Netanyahu as fixated with the Iranian issue: 'If Netanyahu's tone was triumphant, and the smile barely suppressed, it is hardly surprising. He has spent most of his political career obsessed with the threat he believes Iran poses to Israel.'[14] Netanyahu faces long running corruption charges and is in an uneasy alliance with radical groups in his coalition government, so his policies must be motivated by self-interest. *The Guardian* wrote, 'Trust has been broken by the current prime minister, Benjamin Netanyahu, who is using the war to bolster public support for his own political career.'[15] In another opinion piece *The Guardian* wrote, 'Netanyahu is the prime warmonger…Peace is his enemy. Forever war keeps him in power…What Netanyahu really wants is a forever war.'[16] It seems not to dawn on the *Guardian* editor and reporters that what Netanyahu might want (and what the Israeli

public want) are quick decisive wars that defeat the foes that aim at their destruction. It is not only Netanyahu who cares about stopping Iran's race to the bomb, the whole population of Israel does too. The existence of the Jewish state commands consensus in Israel (as the existence of any nation state commands consensus among its population), and the attacks on Iran have virtually universal support.

9. *Israel's astonishing military triumph* Israel, a tiny country the size of Wales, fought a war on seven fronts. It cut Iran down to size, put an end to its position as a Near East superpower. It eliminated the hideous regime of Assad. It more or less destroyed Hezbollah and gave Lebanon a chance to restore its independent statehood. It fought with unparalleled military skills, in the air, on the sea, in daring commando raids, in military intelligence. Its warriors were worthy heirs to the Maccabees in their great war against the Seleucid Macedonians who sought to crush the Jews. But this did not arouse the admiration of the West or lessen the flood of antisemitism among governments, the press and television, mass media, and on the streets of western and antipodean cities. Antisemitism, in the guise of anti-Zionism, is now respectable and widespread, especially among left-wing oriented people and among intellectuals. Antisemitism is not a Jewish problem. It is a problem of western civilization – a moral disease that is now reaching pandemic proportions. But, as I have laboured to make clear, what begins with antisemitism rarely ends there. It is not only an evil in its own right, it is also an omen of social evils that are yet to come. That is why it is important to all decent, clear-thinking people to combat it.

Notes

1 By Center on Extremism; Published: 13 June 2025 by the Anti Defamation League. Available at www.adl.org/resources/article/escalation-between-isr ael-iranian-regime-sparks-vicious-antisemitic-anti-israel

2 By Summer Said, Dov Lieber and Benoit Faucon; Published: 25 October 2023 by the Wall Street Journal. Available at www.wsj.com/world/middle-east/hamas-fighters-trained-in-iran-before-oct-7-attacks-e2a8dbb9

3 By Jennifer McKiernan; Published: 13 June 2025 by the BBC. Available at www.bbc.co.uk/news/articles/c1ld0n8m4lro

4 By *ANP* and *NL Times*; Published: 13 June 2025 by the *NL Times*. Available at https://nltimes.nl/2025/06/13/dutch-pm-urges-restraint-israel-iran-att ack-tehran-klm-cancels-flight

5 By Henry Samuel; Published: 23 June 2025 by *The Telegraph*. Available at www.telegraph.co.uk/world-news/2025/06/23/macron-trump-air-stri kes-against-iran-illegal/

6 By James Angelos; Published: 20 June 2025 by Politico. Available at www.politico.eu/newsletter/berlin-bulletin/merzs-dirty-work/

7 By Simon Plosker; Published: 24 June 2025 by Ynet Global. Available at www.ynetnews.com/article/h1n117tweex

8 By Jon Holmes and Dead Ringers; Published: 20 June 2025 by BBC. Available at www.bbc.co.uk/sounds/play/p0ljglyw

9 By Gil Hoffman; Published: 29 June 2025 by *The Jerusalem Post*. Available at www.jpost.com/opinion/article-859100

10 By Jonathan Swan and Maggie Haberman; Published: 21 June 2025 by *The New York Times*. Available at www.nytimes.com/2025/06/21/world/ middleeast/us-bomb-iran-trump-war.html

11 By Jo Floto; Published: 22 June 2025 by BBC. Available at www.bbc. co.uk/news/articles/c9dgpjqg12lo

12 By Sahar Maranlou; Published: 20 June 2025 by The Conversation. Available at https://theconversation.com/who-is-irans-leader-ayatollah-ali-khamenei-259424

13 By unnamed; Published: 21 June 2025 by *The Economist*. Available at www.economist.com/middle-east-and-africa/2025/06/21/ayatollah-ali-khamenei-irans-great-survivor

14 By Jo Floto; Published: 22 June 2025 by BBC. Available at www.bbc. co.uk/news/articles/c9dgpjqg12lo

15 By Nesrine Malik; Published: 16 June 2025 by *The Guardian*. Available at www.theguardian.com/commentisfree/2025/jun/16/gaza-israel-destro yed-reputation-attacking-iran-benjamin-netanyahu

16 By Simon Tisdall; Published: 29 June 2025 by *The Guardian*. Available at www.theguardian.com/commentisfree/2025/jun/29/iran-israel-ceasefire-netanyahu-forever-war

Maps

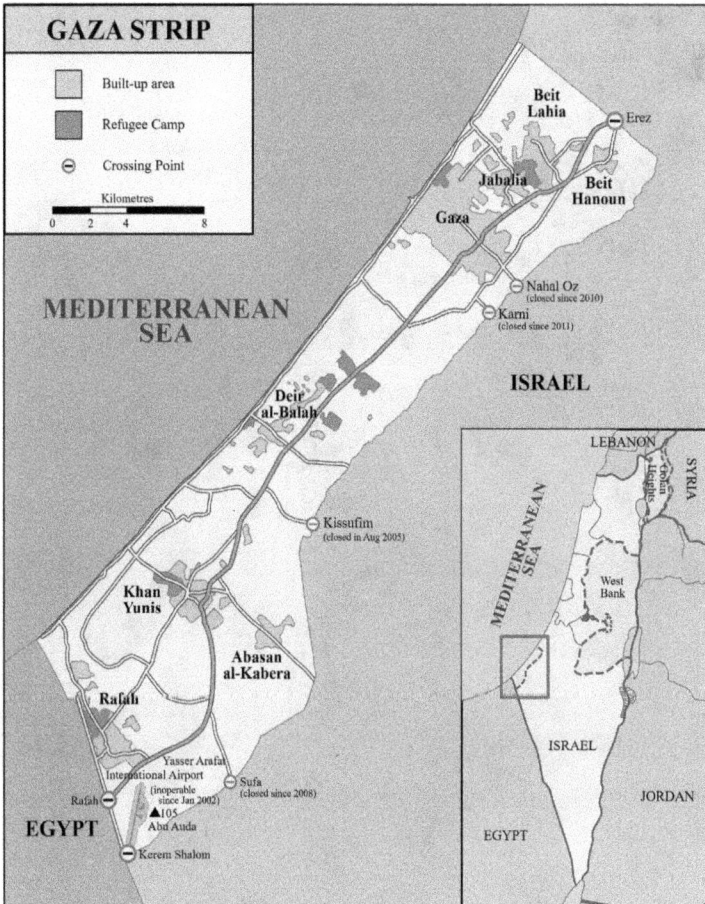

Map 1 Map of the Gaza Strip.

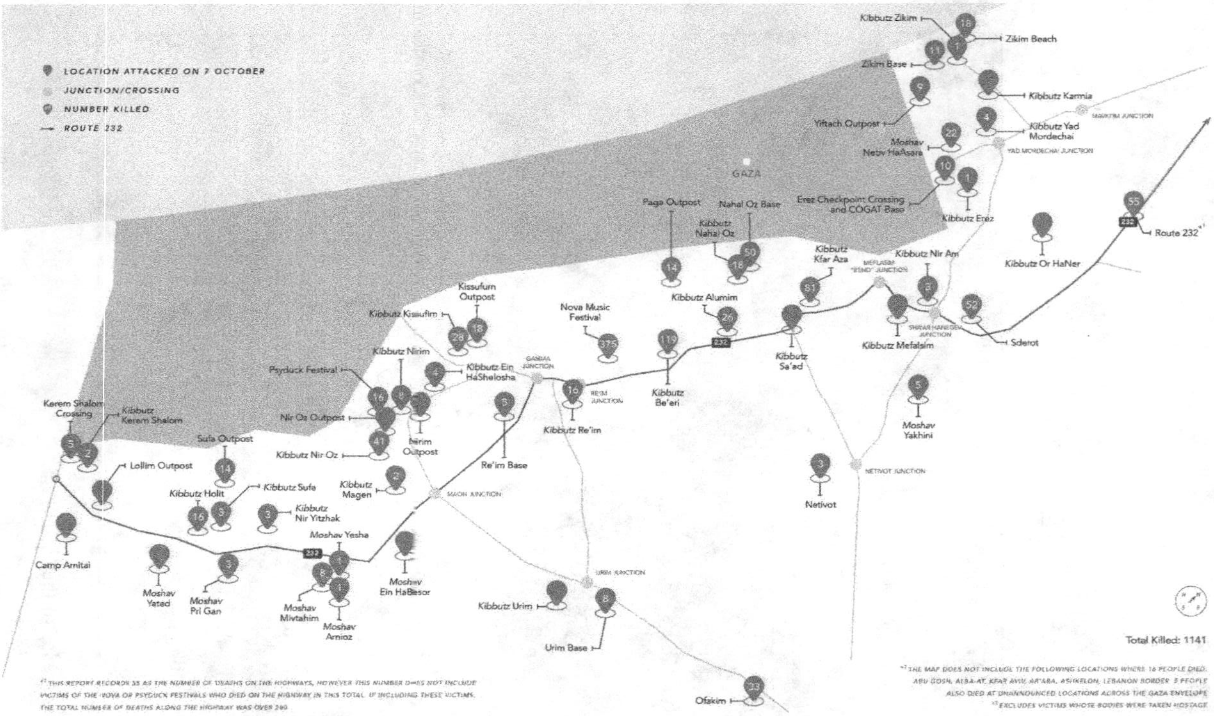

Map 2 Andrew Robert's Map of the Hamas massacre, October 7, 2023.

Source: Figure reproduced with permission from the All Party Parliamentary Group on UK–Israel 7 October Parliamentary Commission Report, chaired by Lord Roberts of Belgravia, (2025).

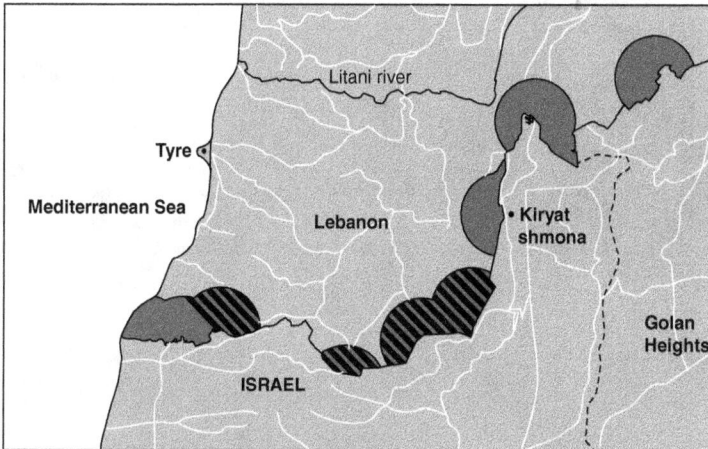

Areas on the Israel-Lebanon boundary from which Hezbollah fired anti-tank missiles from Oct. 8, 2023

Map 3 Areas on the Israel-Lebanon boundary from which Hezbollah fired anti-tank missiles at the IDF tank corps from October 8, 2023.

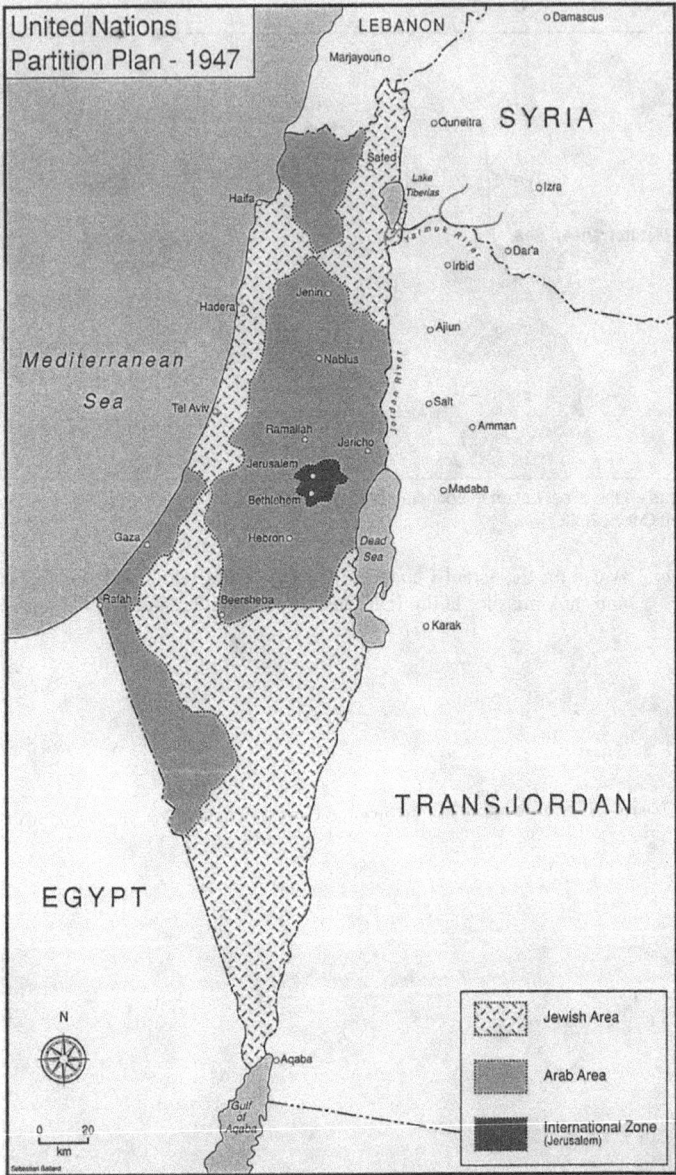

Map 4 United Nations Map of proposed division of the Palestine Mandate 1947.

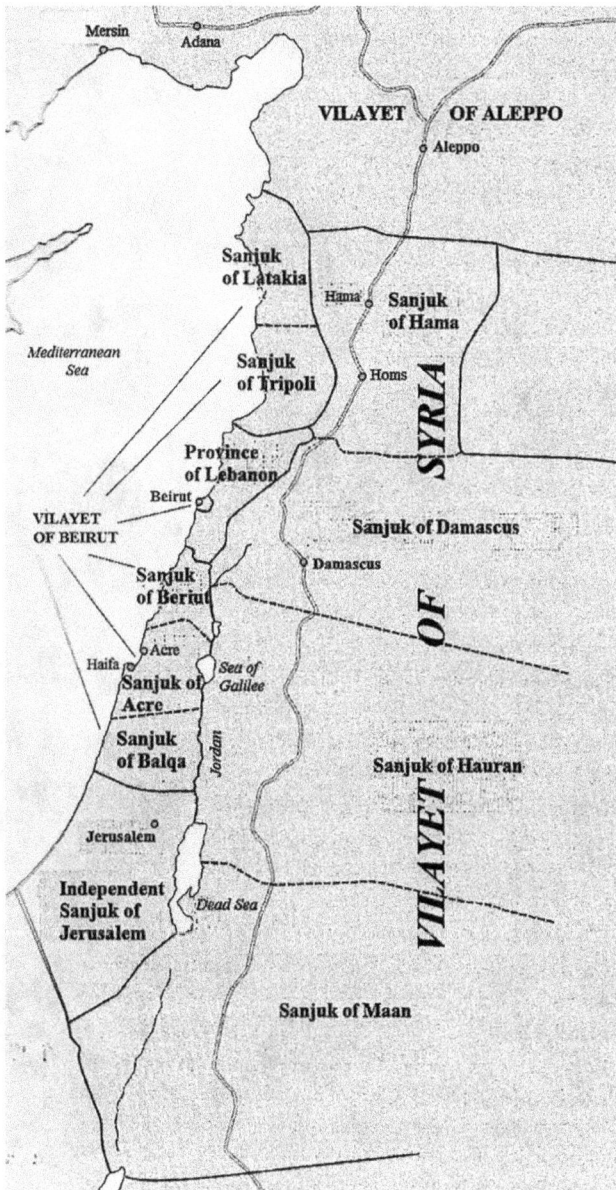

Map 5 Map of the Ottoman Levant 1914.

Source: Public Domain (https://picryl.com/media/ottoman-levant-d0c88c).

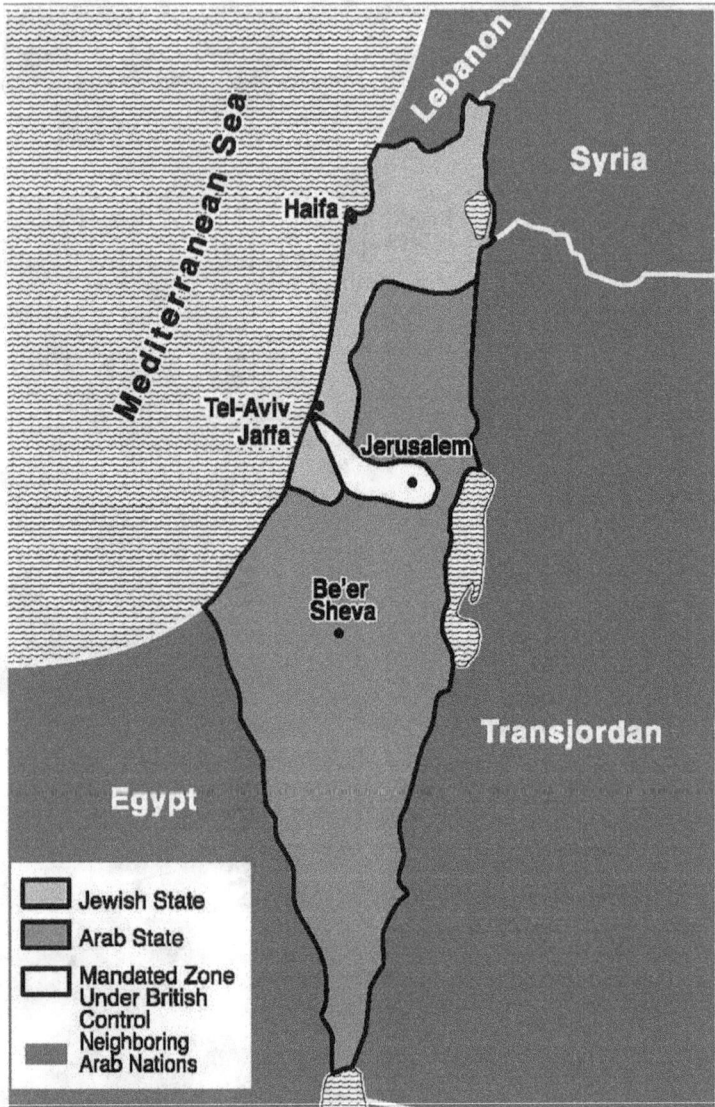

Map 6 Map of the Peel Commission Partition Plan 1937.

Source: The American Israel Cooperative Enterprise, at The Jewish Virtual Library. Reproduced with permission.

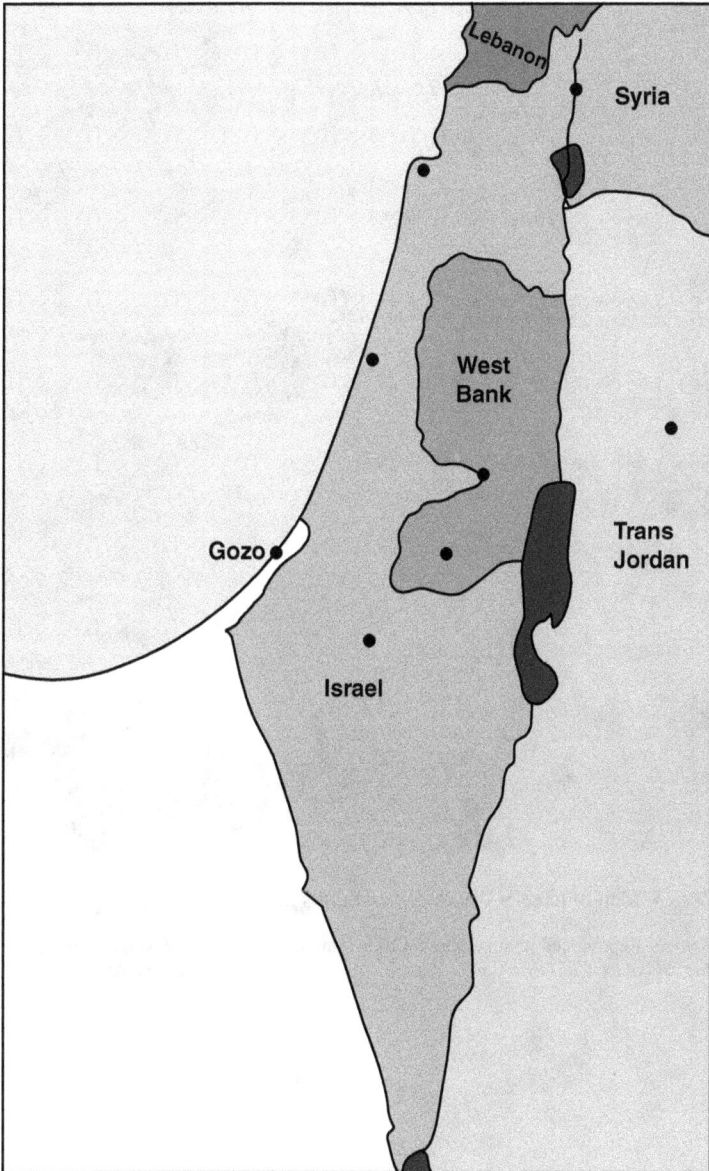

Map 7 Map of Israel: Armistice Lines 1949.

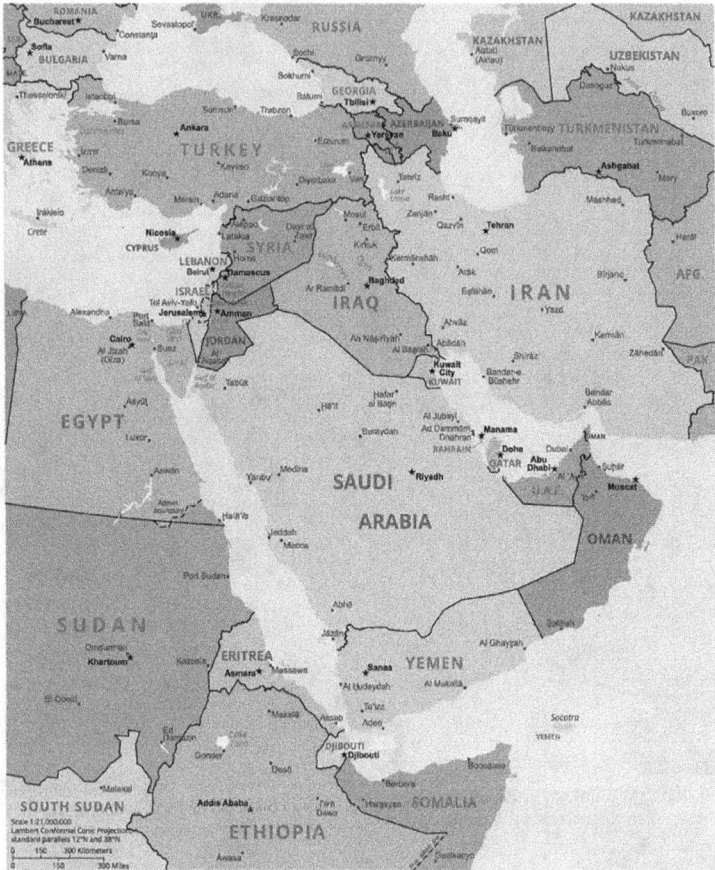

Map 8 Map of Israel's War on Seven Fronts 2023–5.

Source: Reproduced with permission from Amnon Aran, *Israeli Foreign Policy since the End of the Cold War,* Cambridge University Press, 2020. © Amnon Aran.

Index

For Product Safety Concerns and Information please contact our EU
representative GPSR@taylorandfrancis.com
Taylor & Francis Verlag GmbH, Kaufingerstraße 24, 80331 München, Germany